Majestic Mandala

Adult Coloring Book for A Peaceful Soul

Volume 2

I hope you enjoy coloring these Mandalas, as much as I enjoy creating them.
Please remember to breathe and take your time, and don't forget
to take a picture of your final artwork and post it to our facebook page.

I will continue to make my heart happy by creating these designs,
as long as you keep coloring them. Thank you so much for purchasing a copy.

Your contribution will help me fund the raising of my family.
That is why I dedicate this book to them; My beautiful wife and my 3 sons.
Thank you Naomi, Jonah, Kael and Logan for letting me follow my Heart!

ISBN 978-1-5430-0586-8   US$6.95

ISBN; 978-1-5430-0586-8

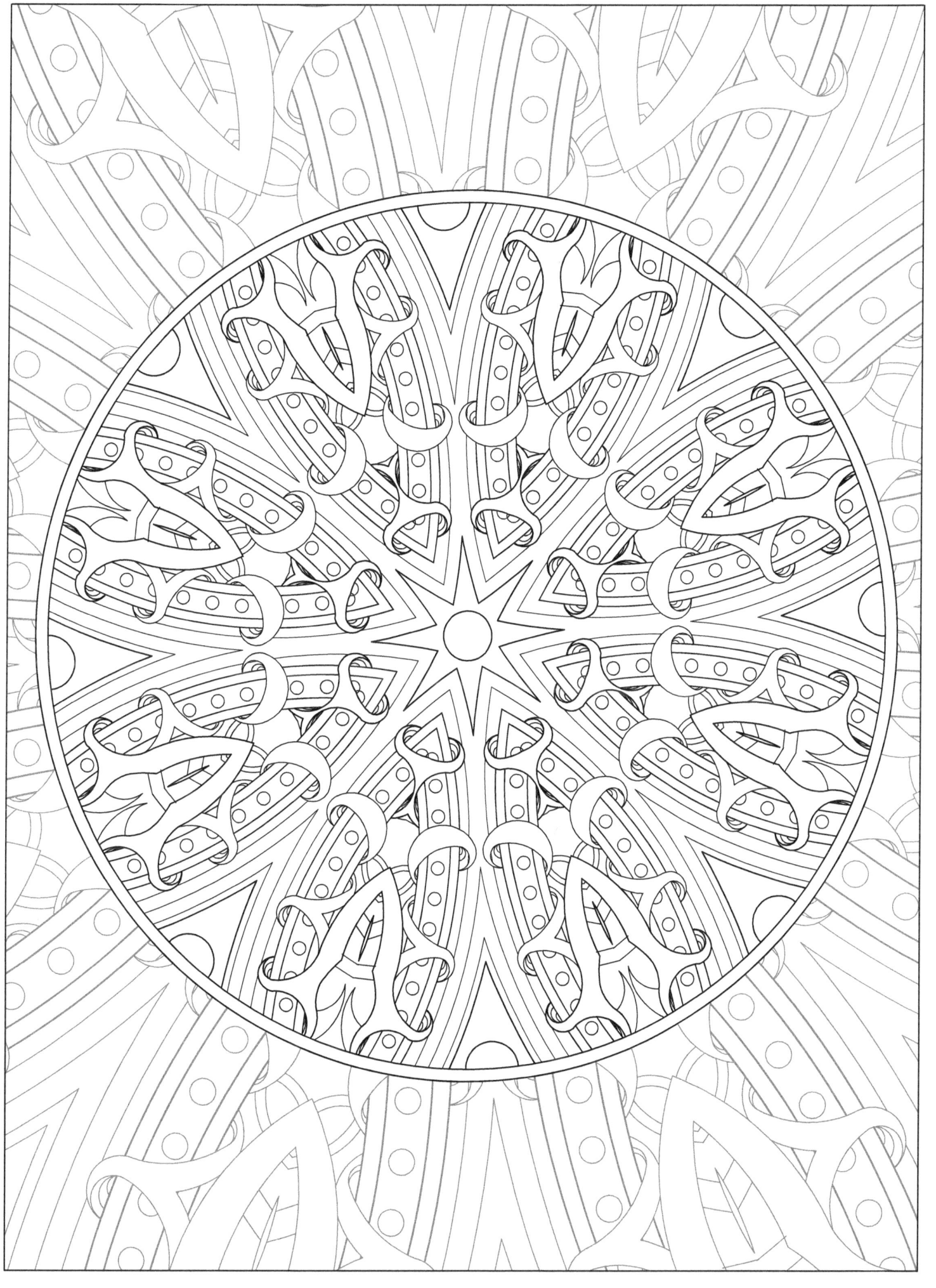

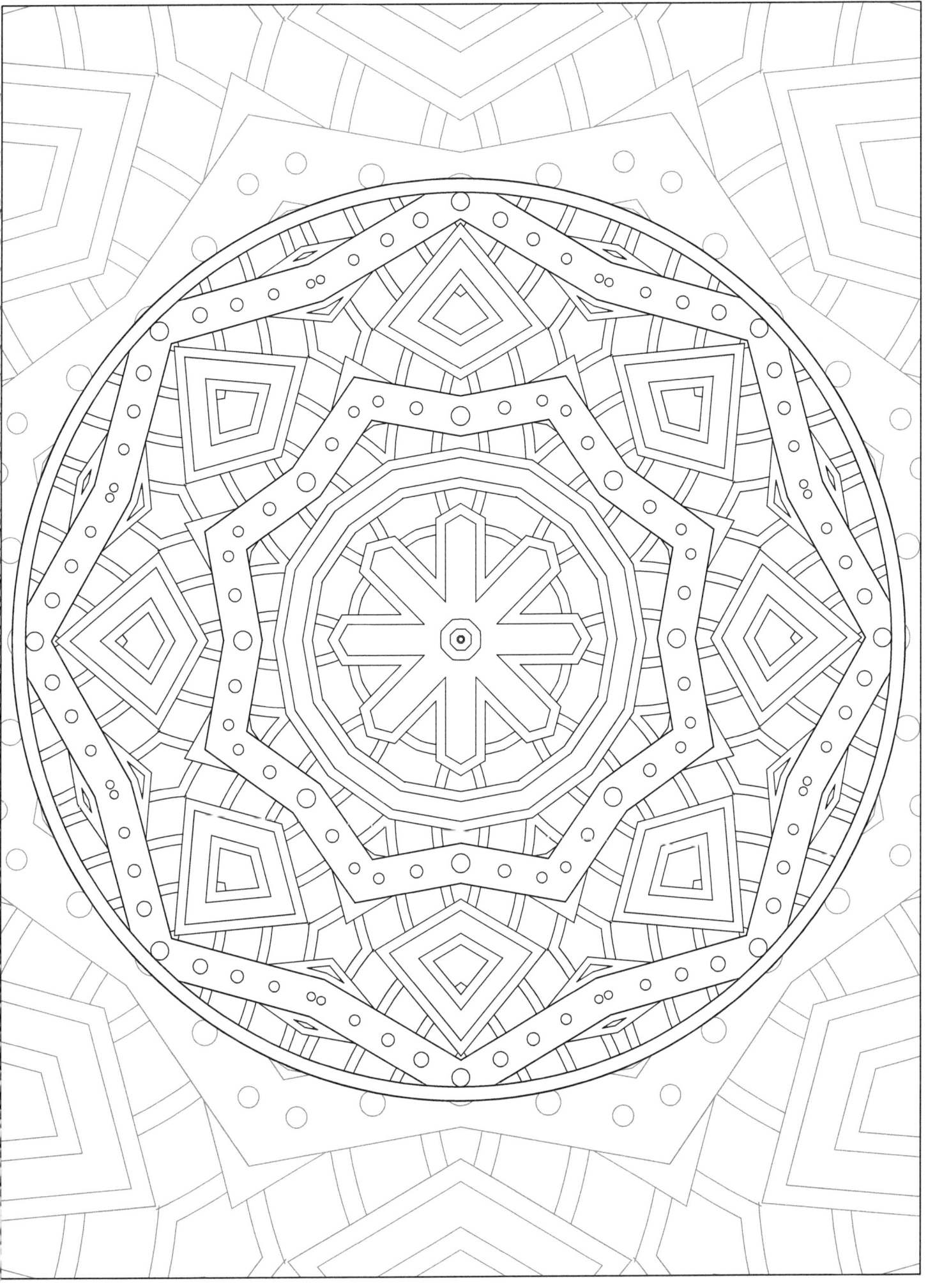

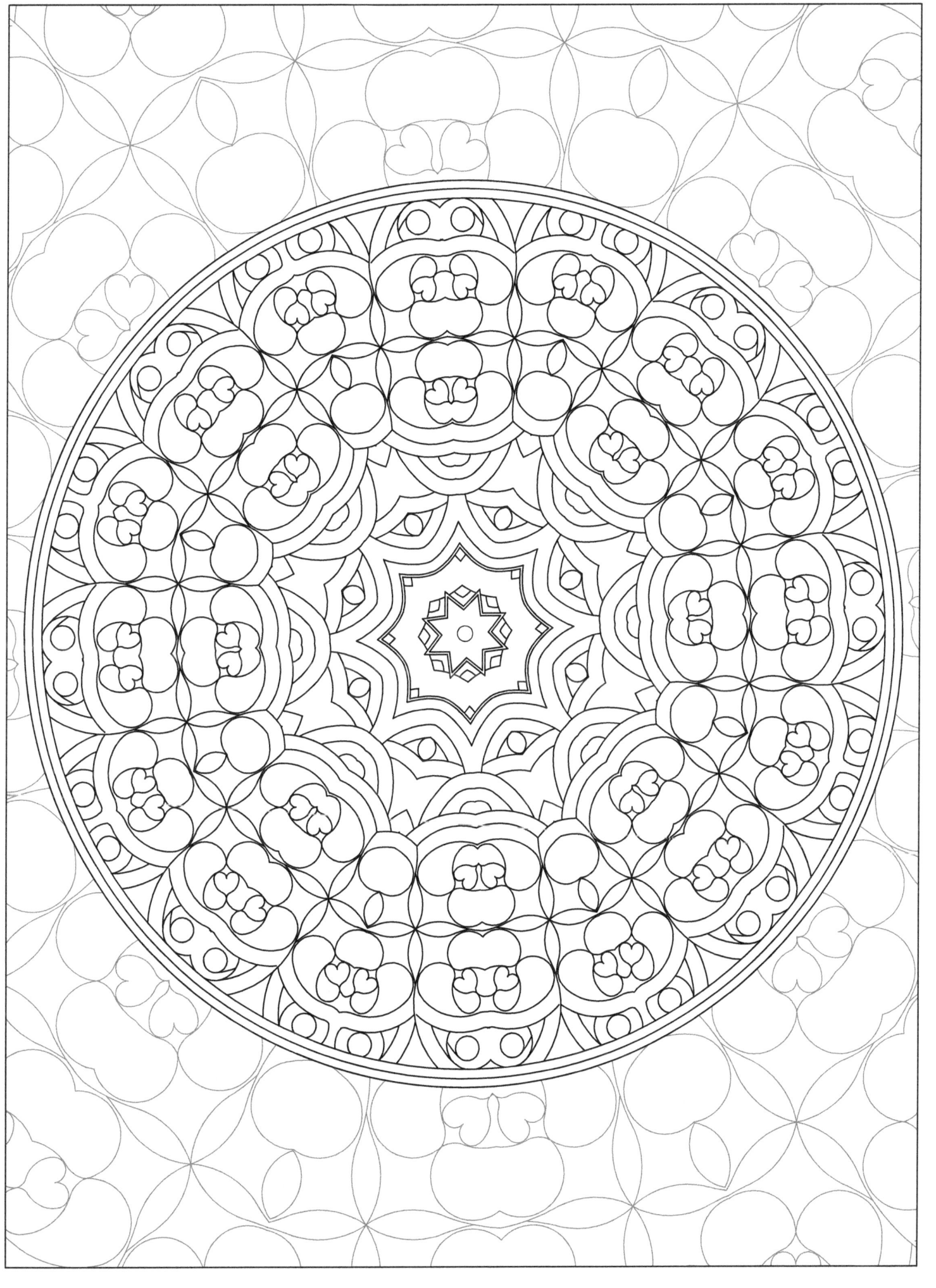

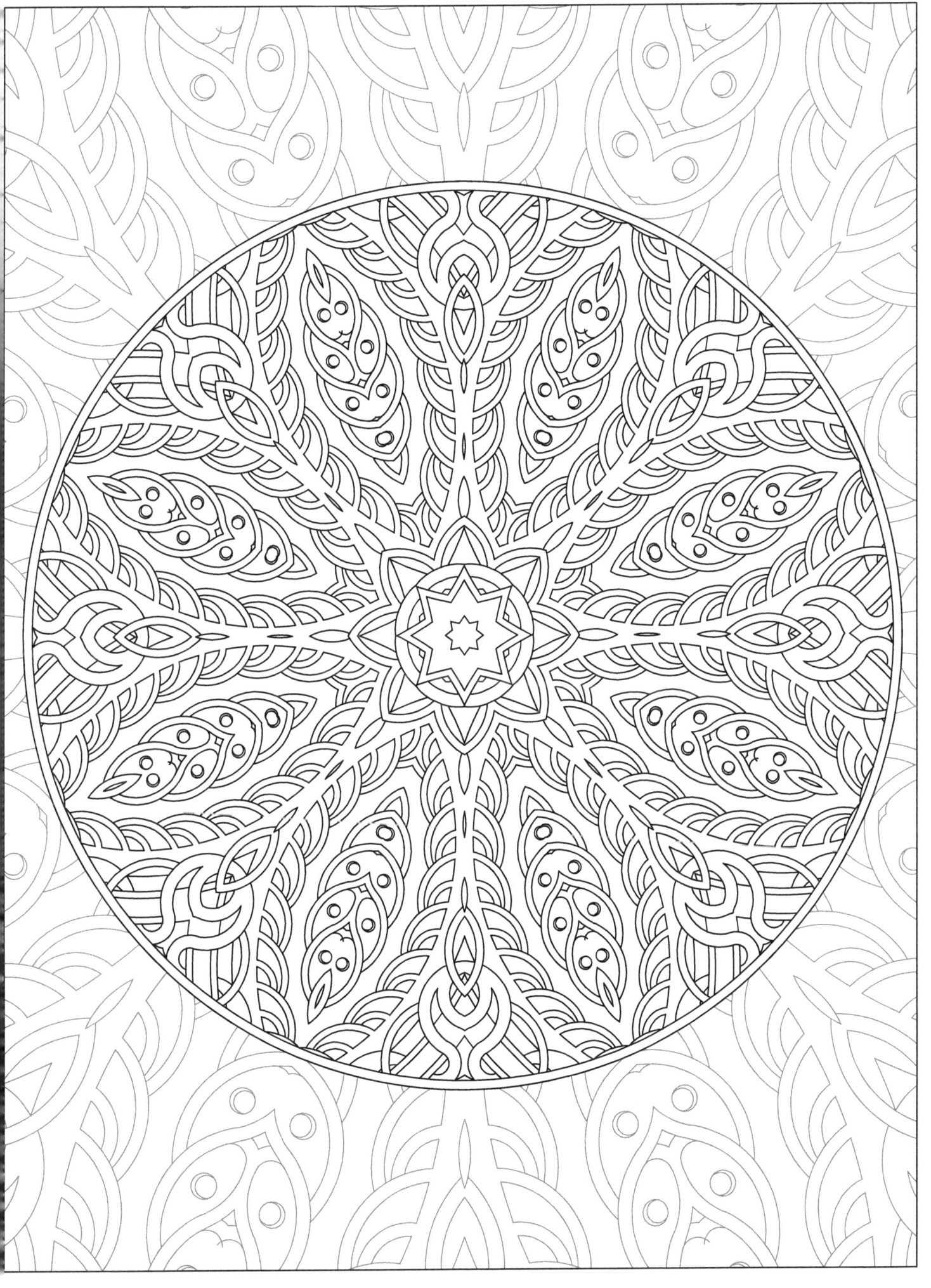

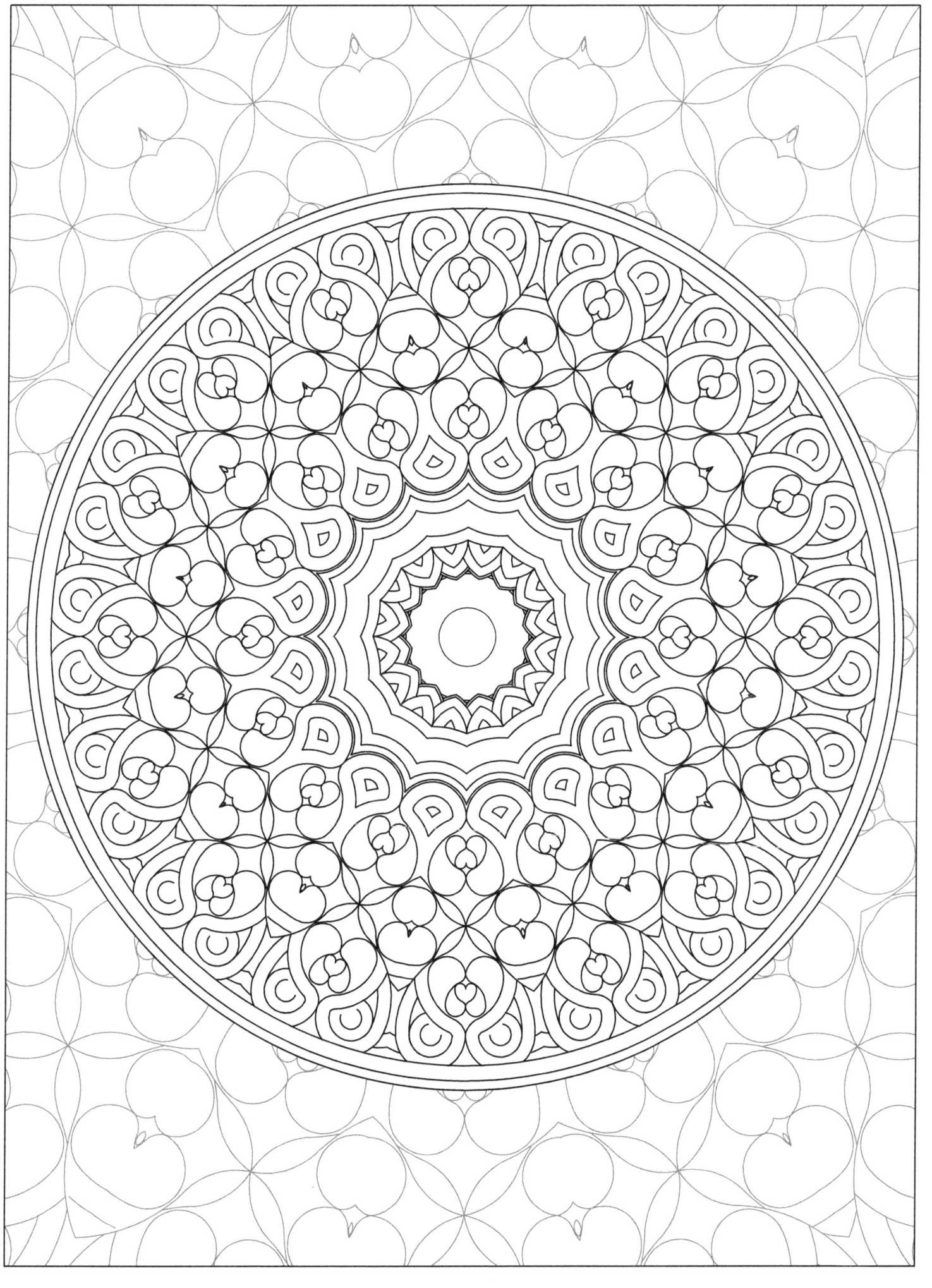

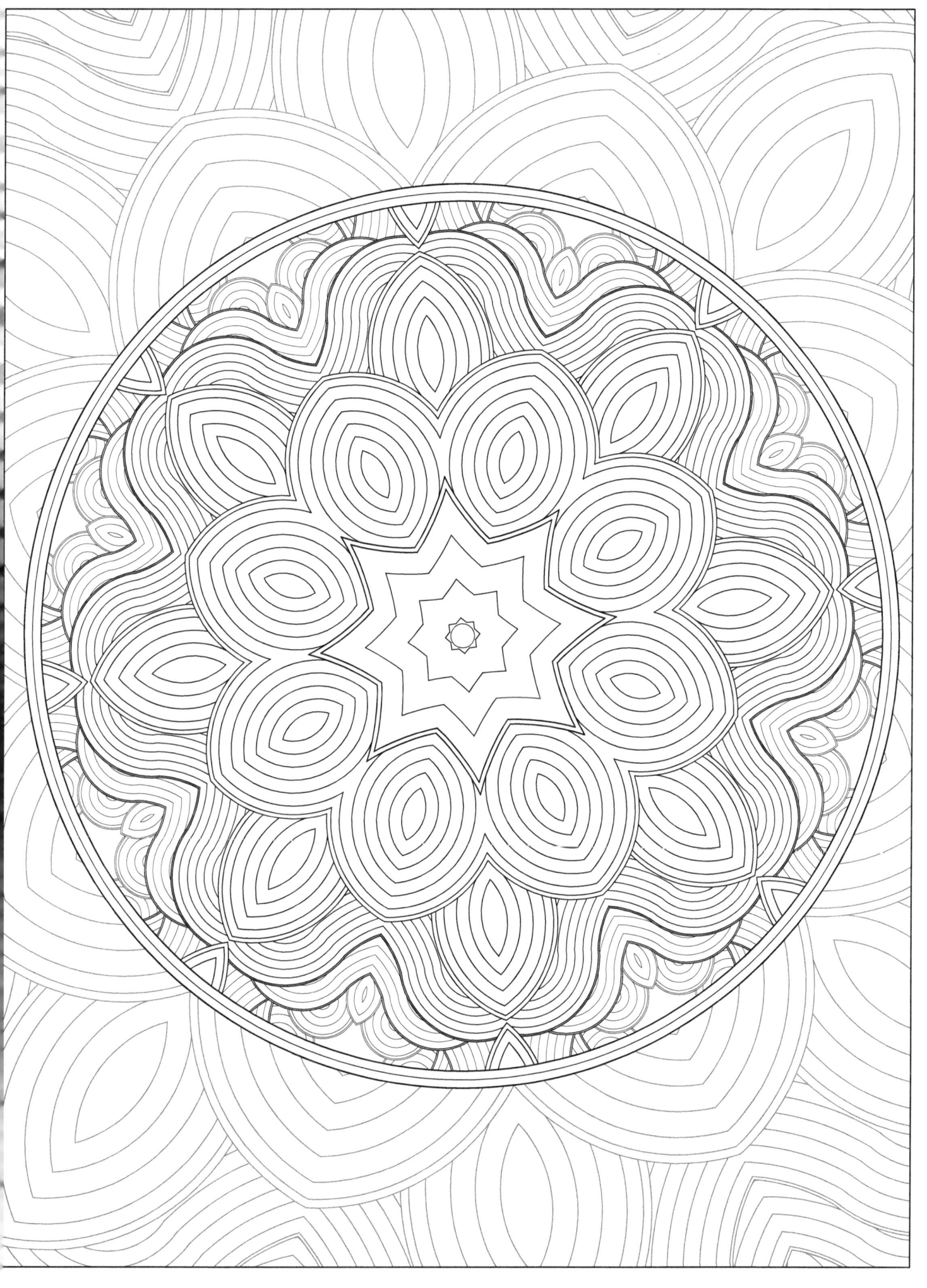

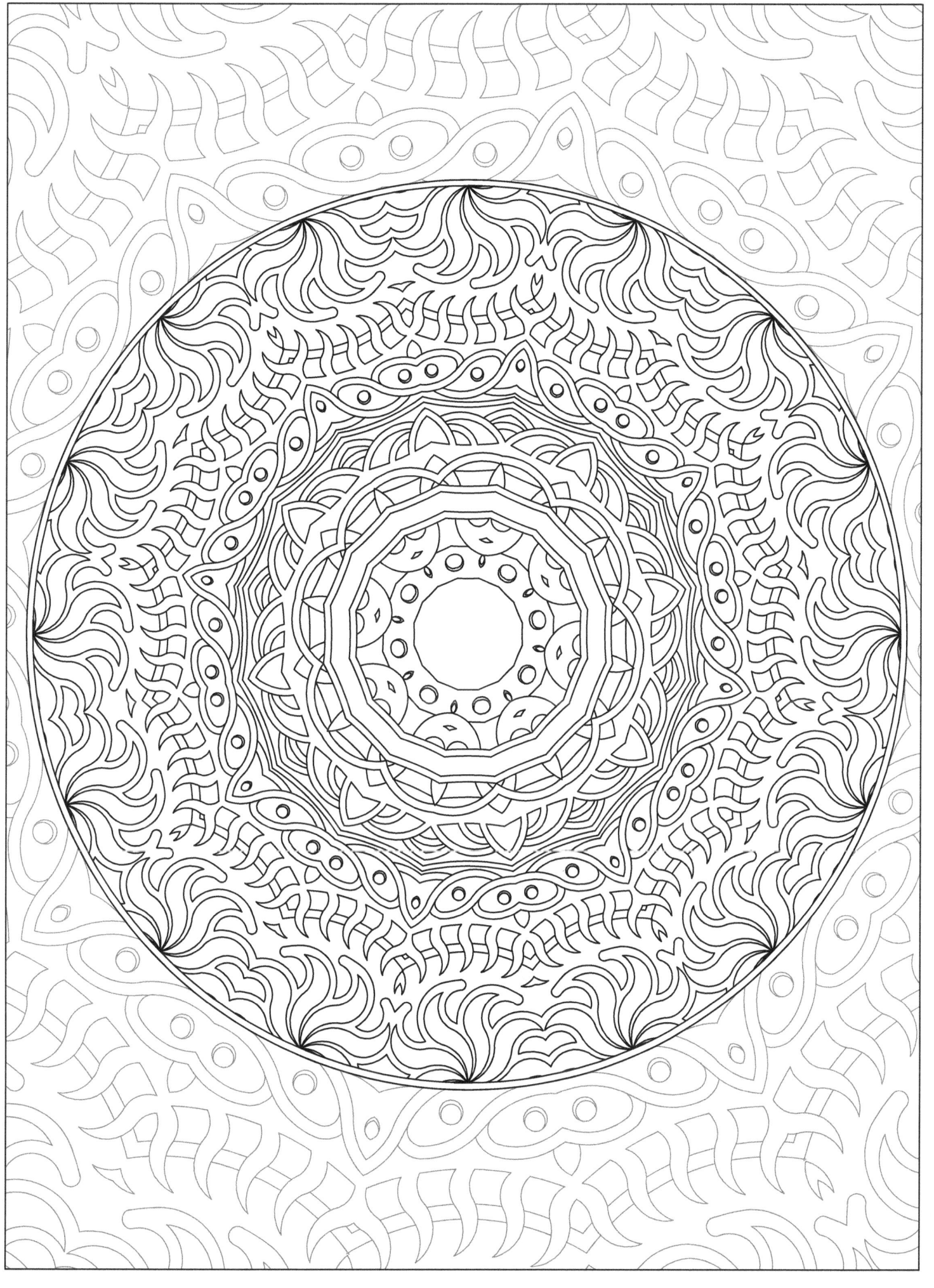

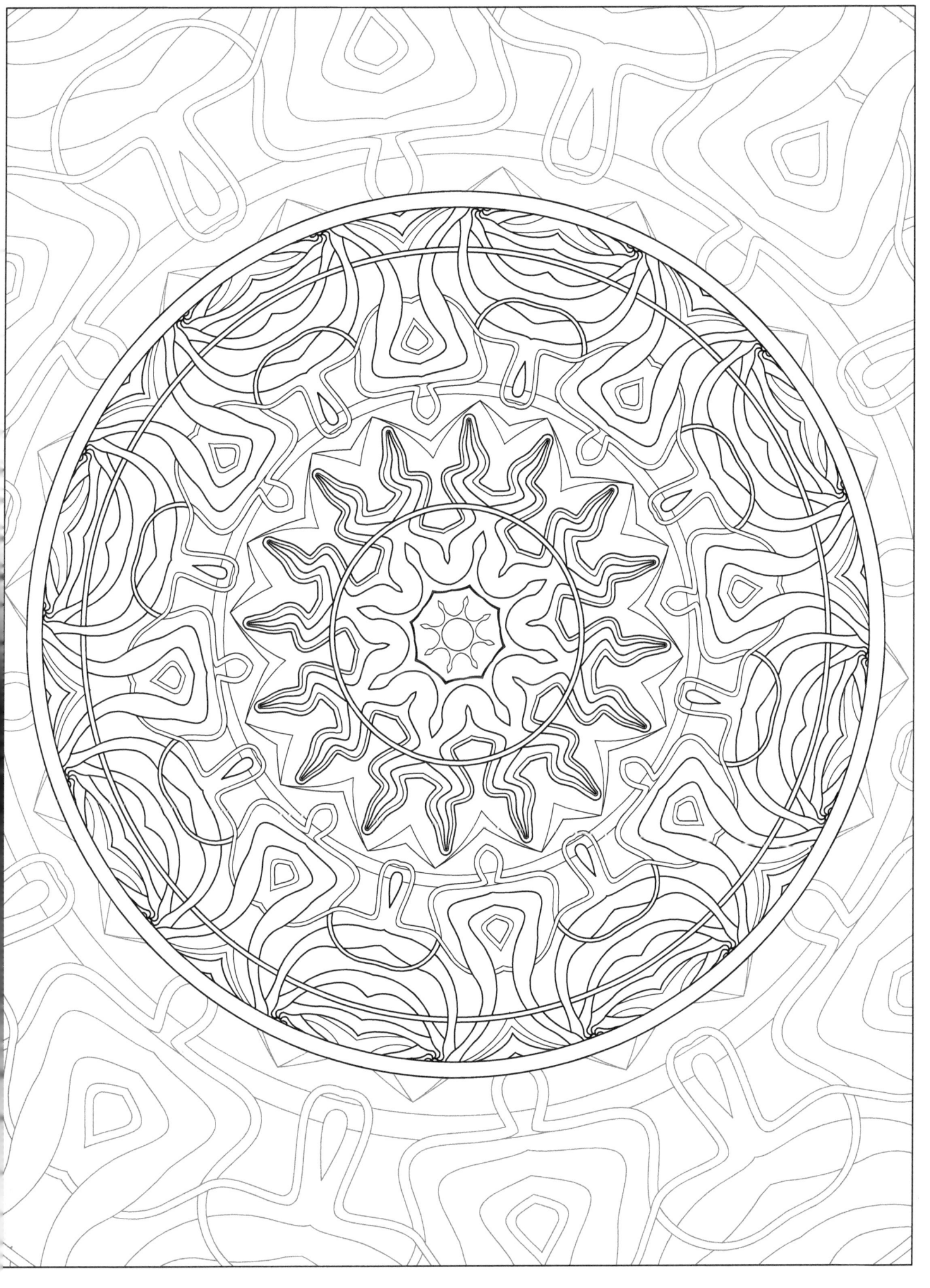

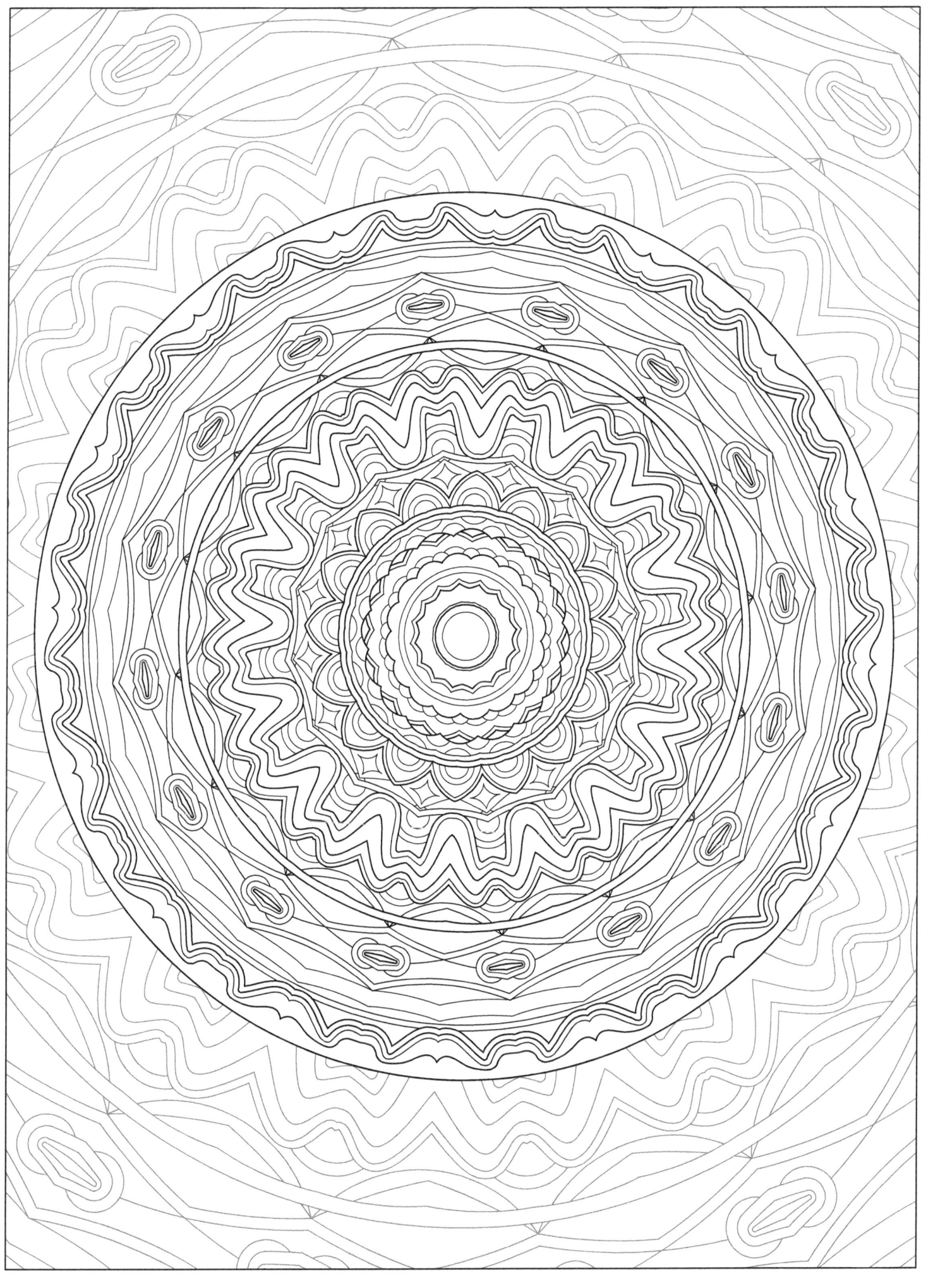

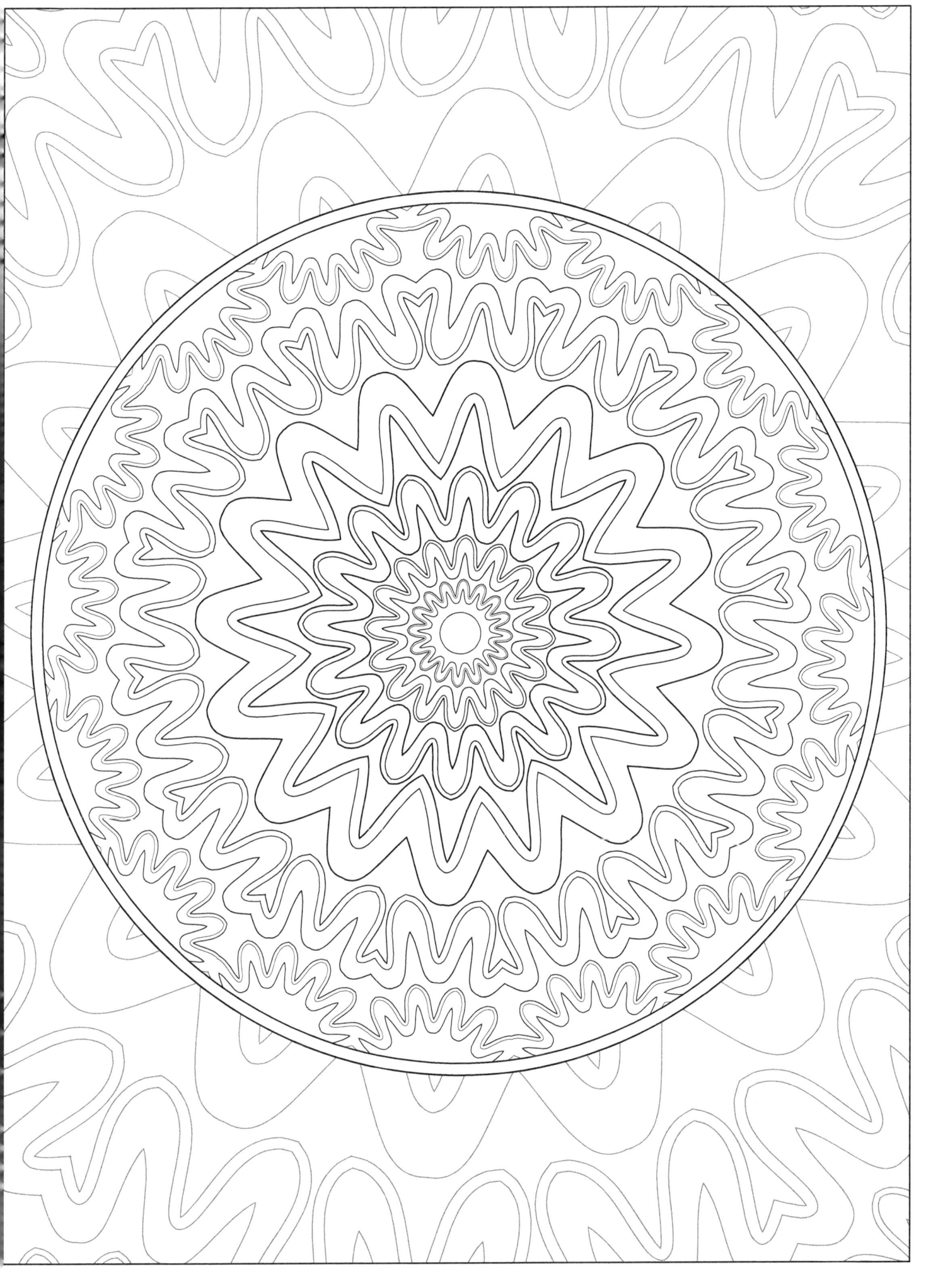

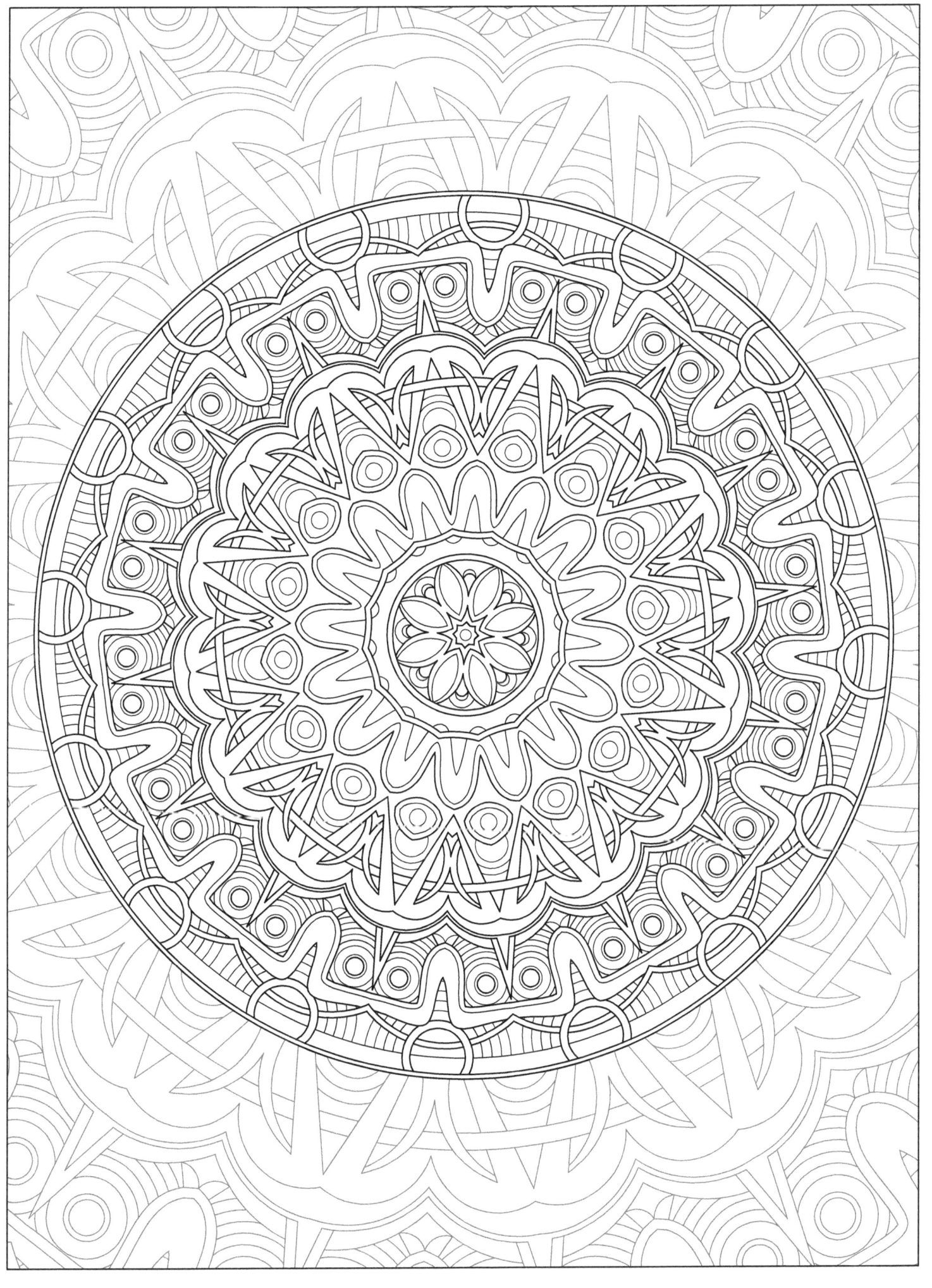

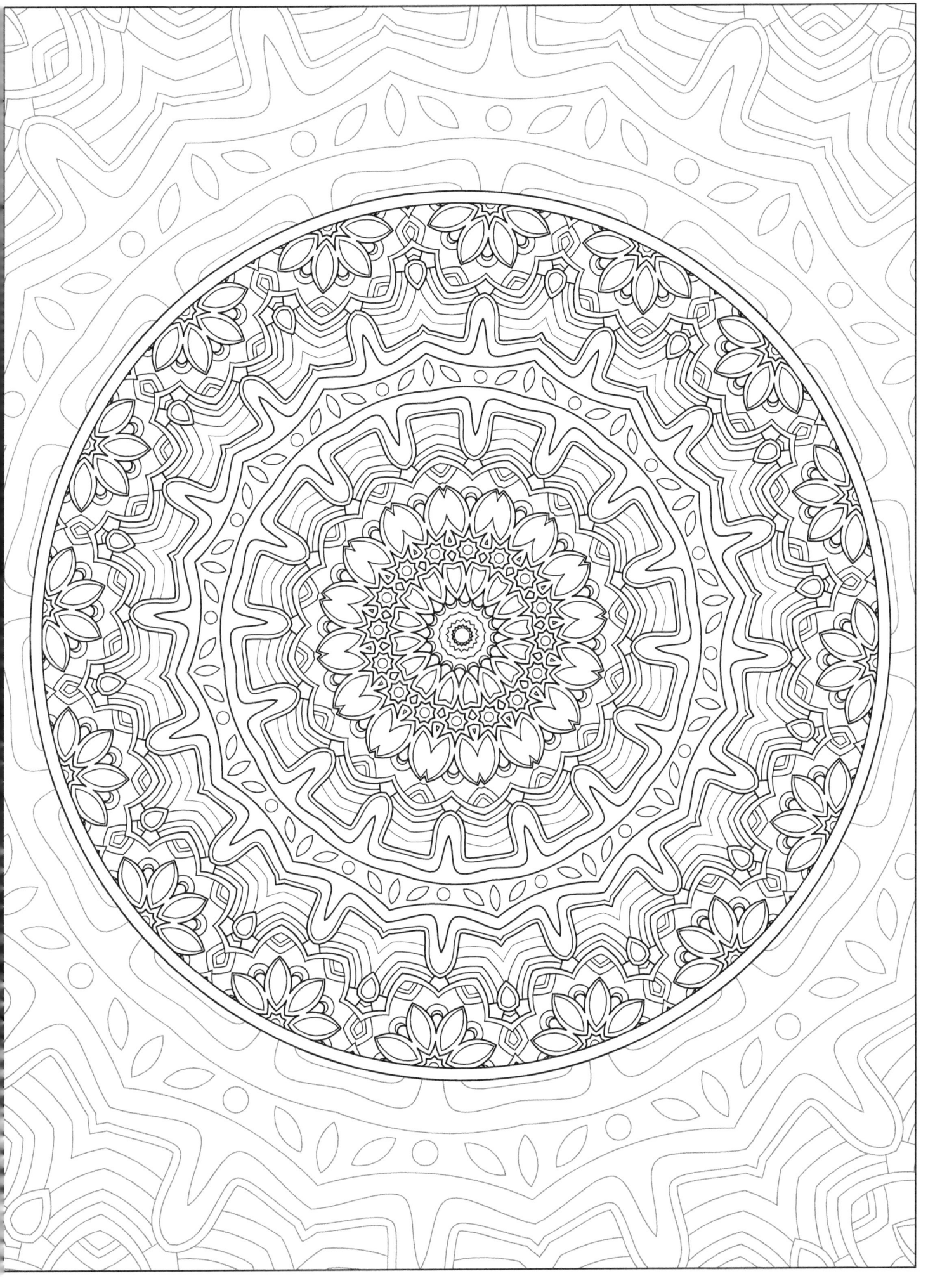

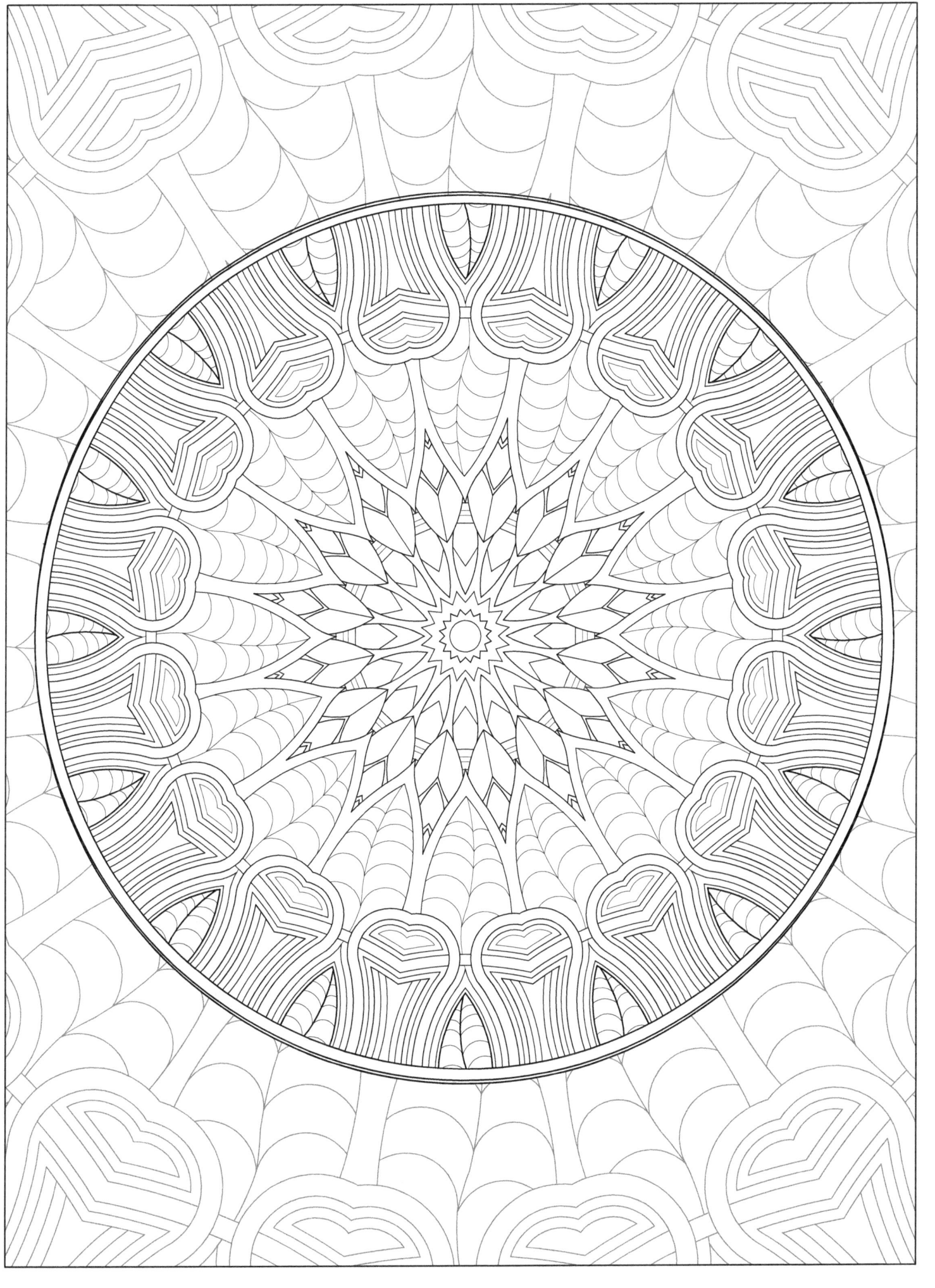

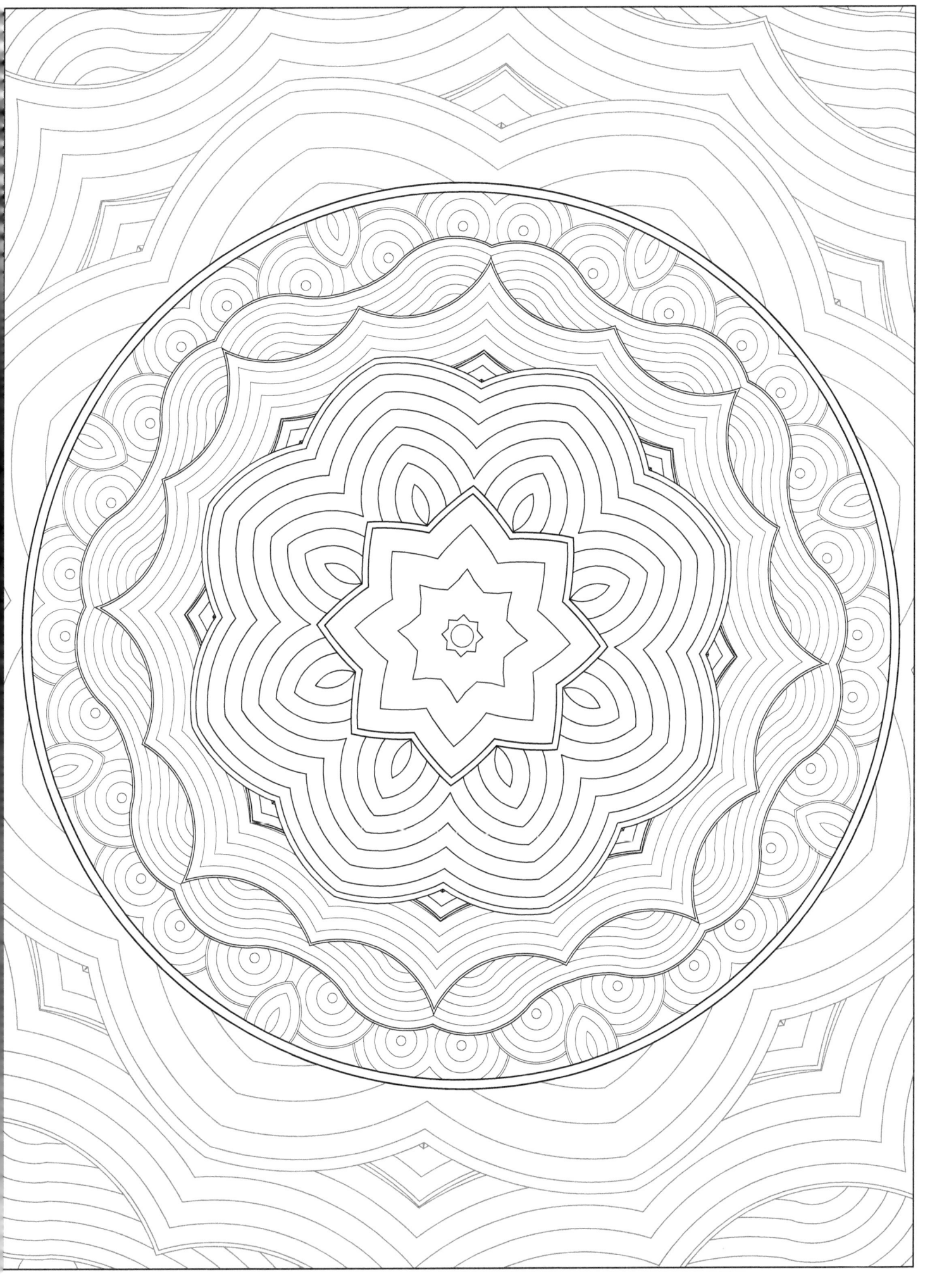

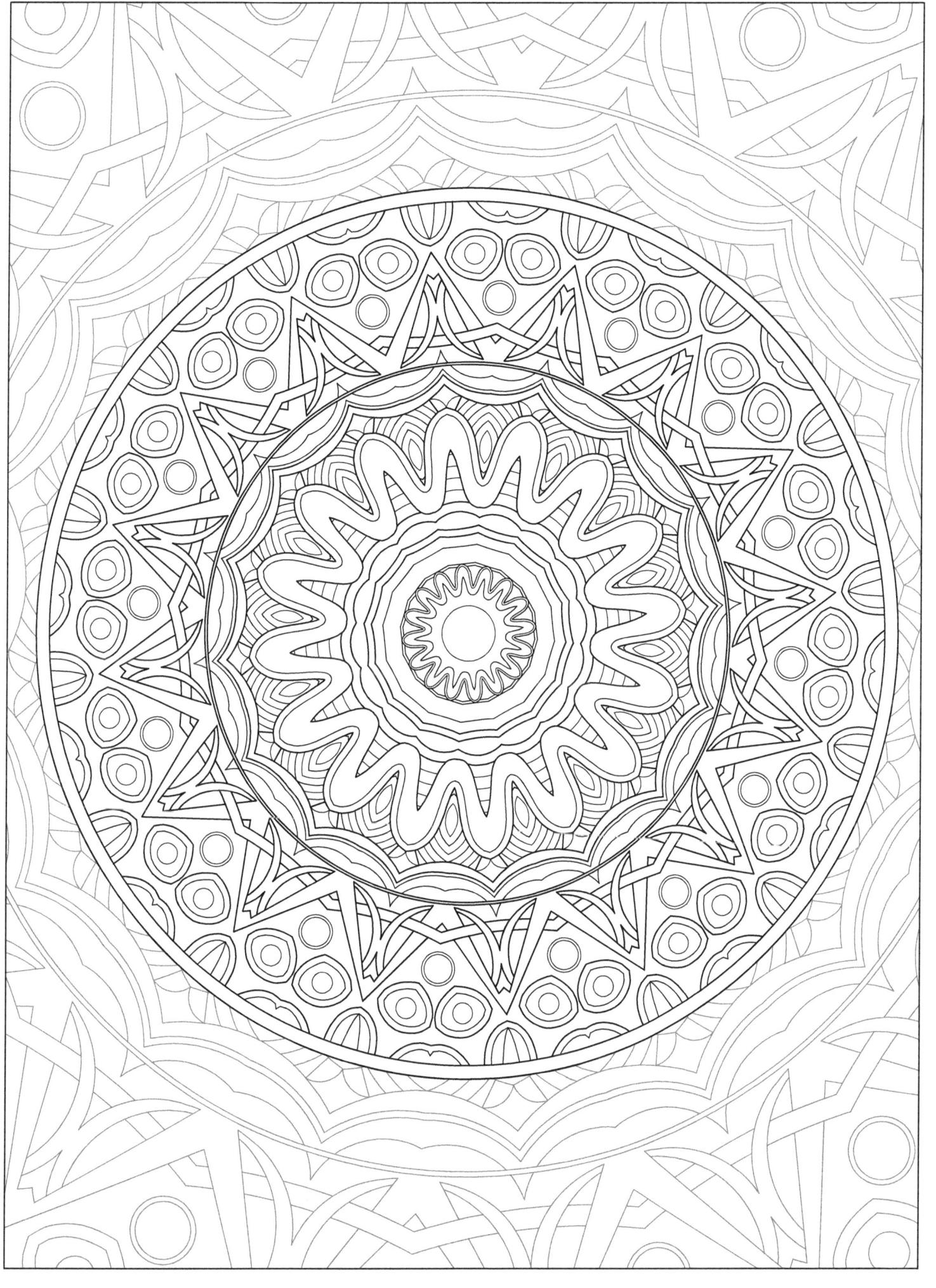

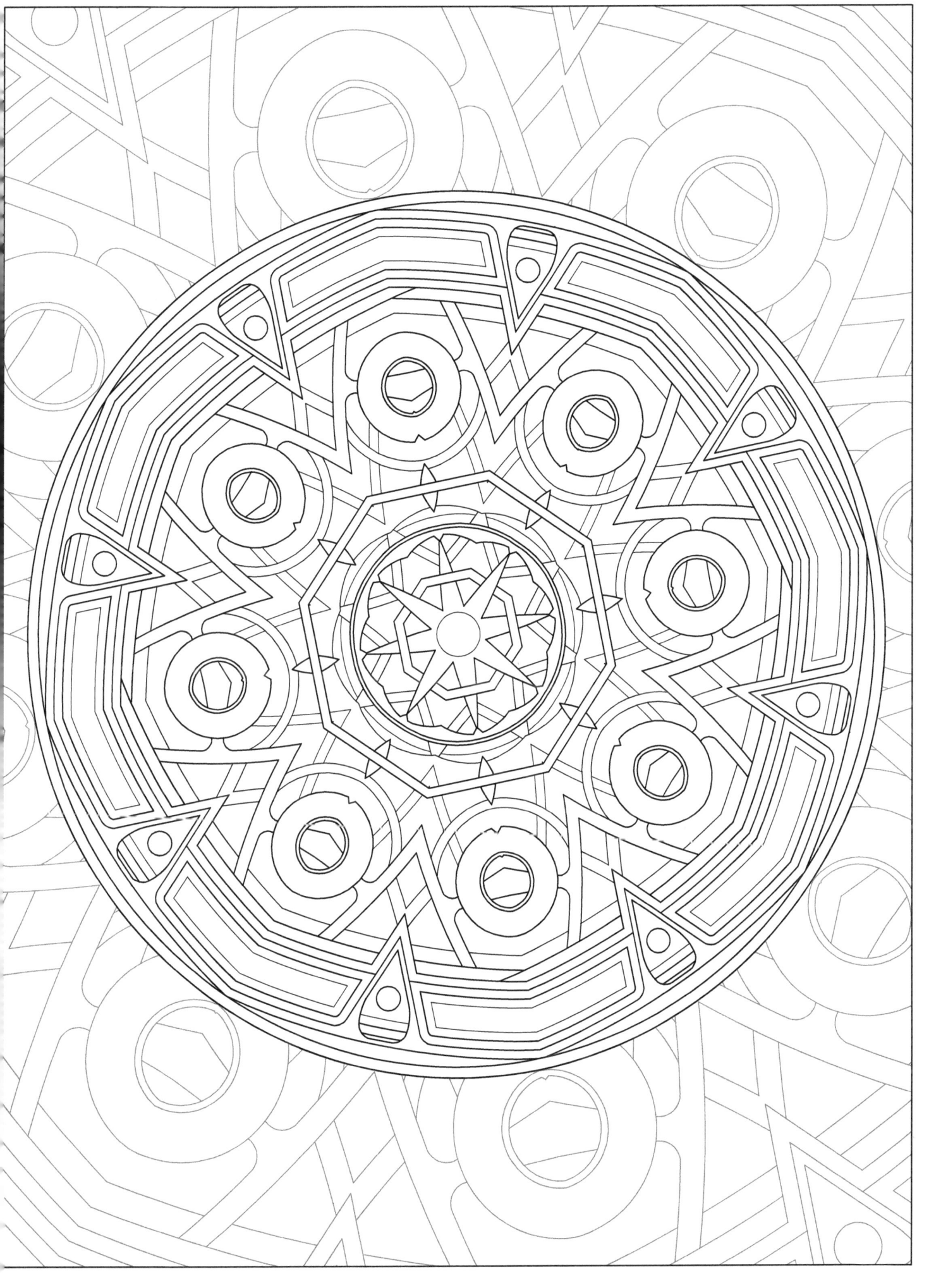

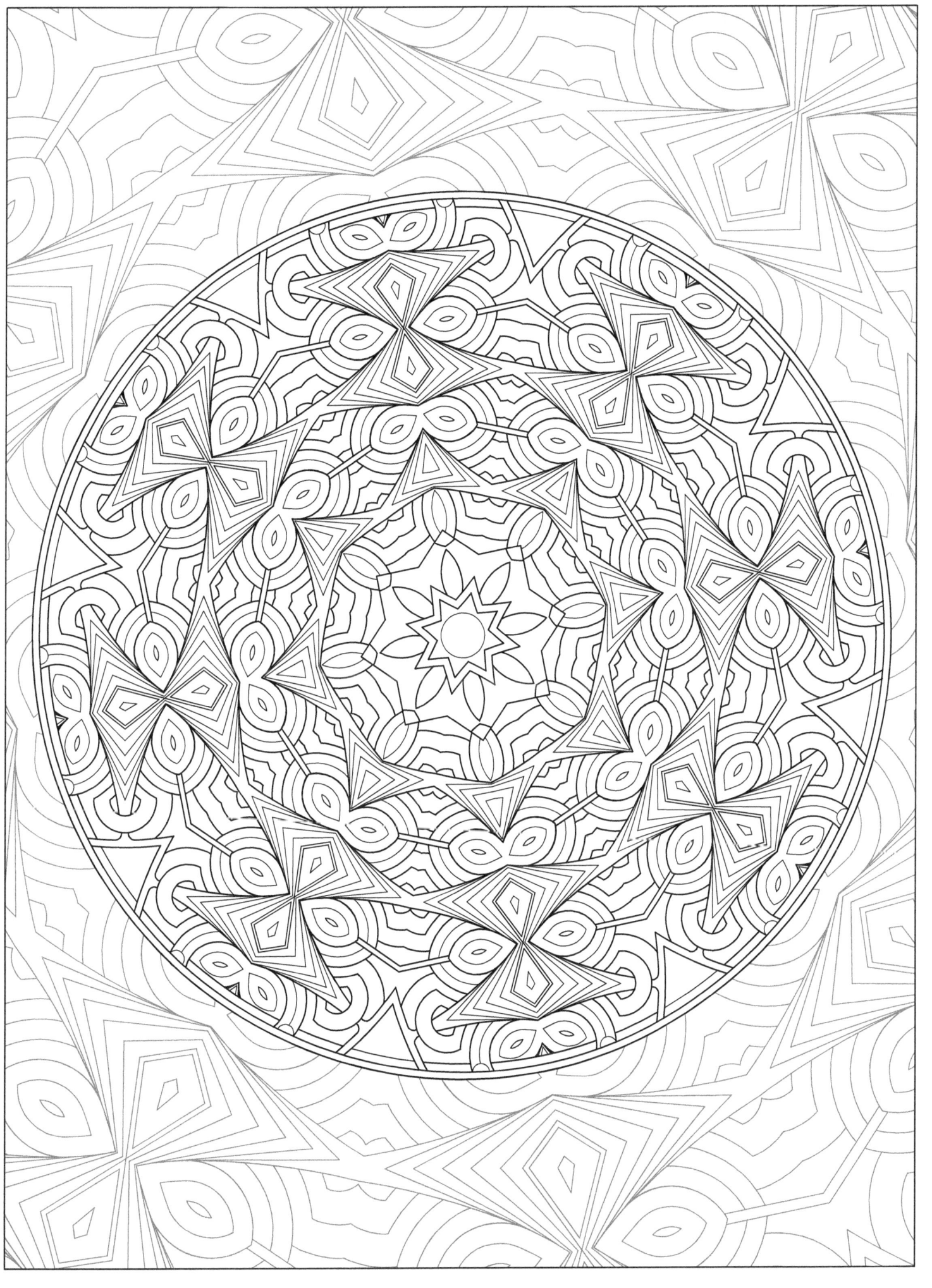

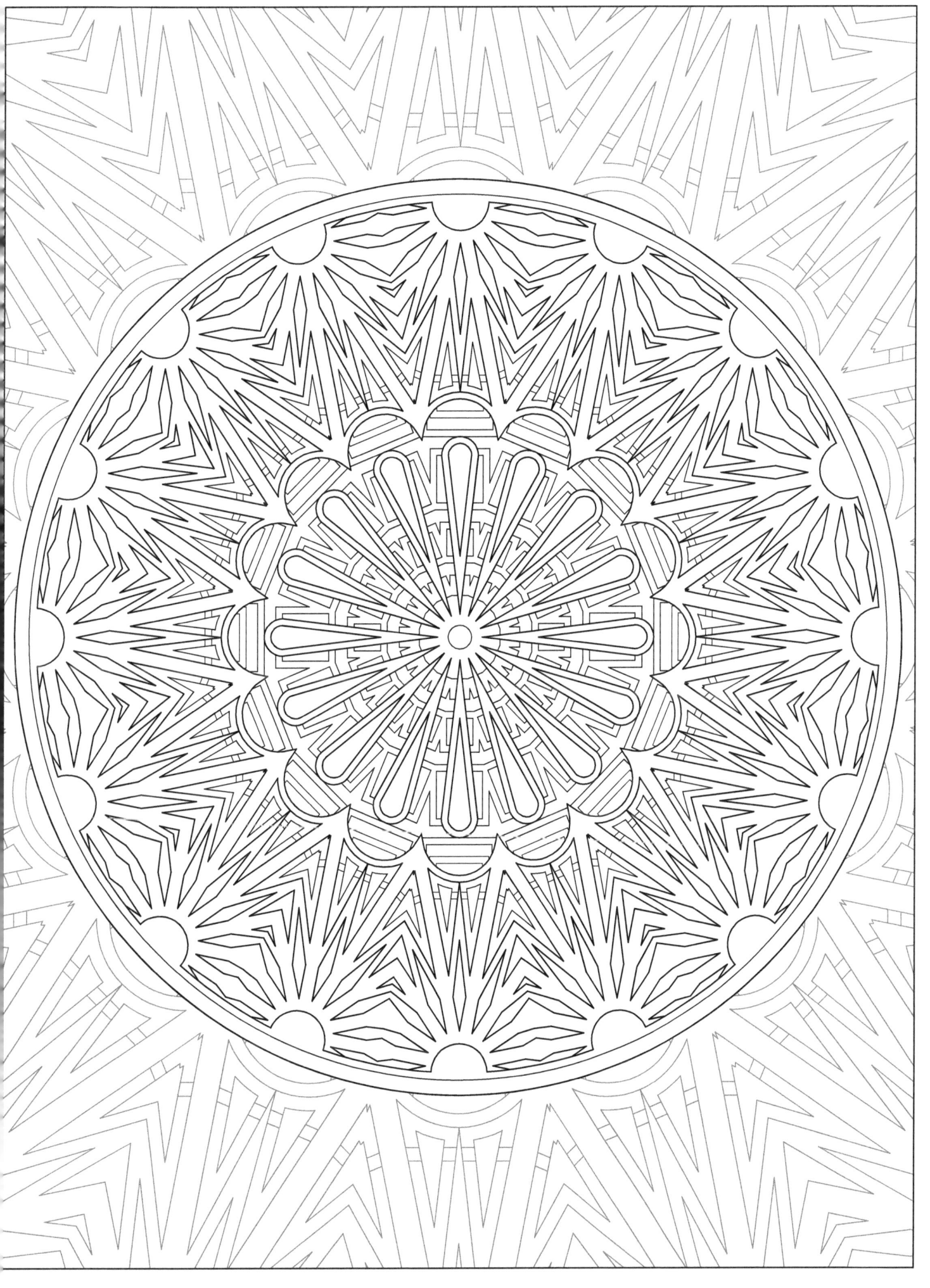

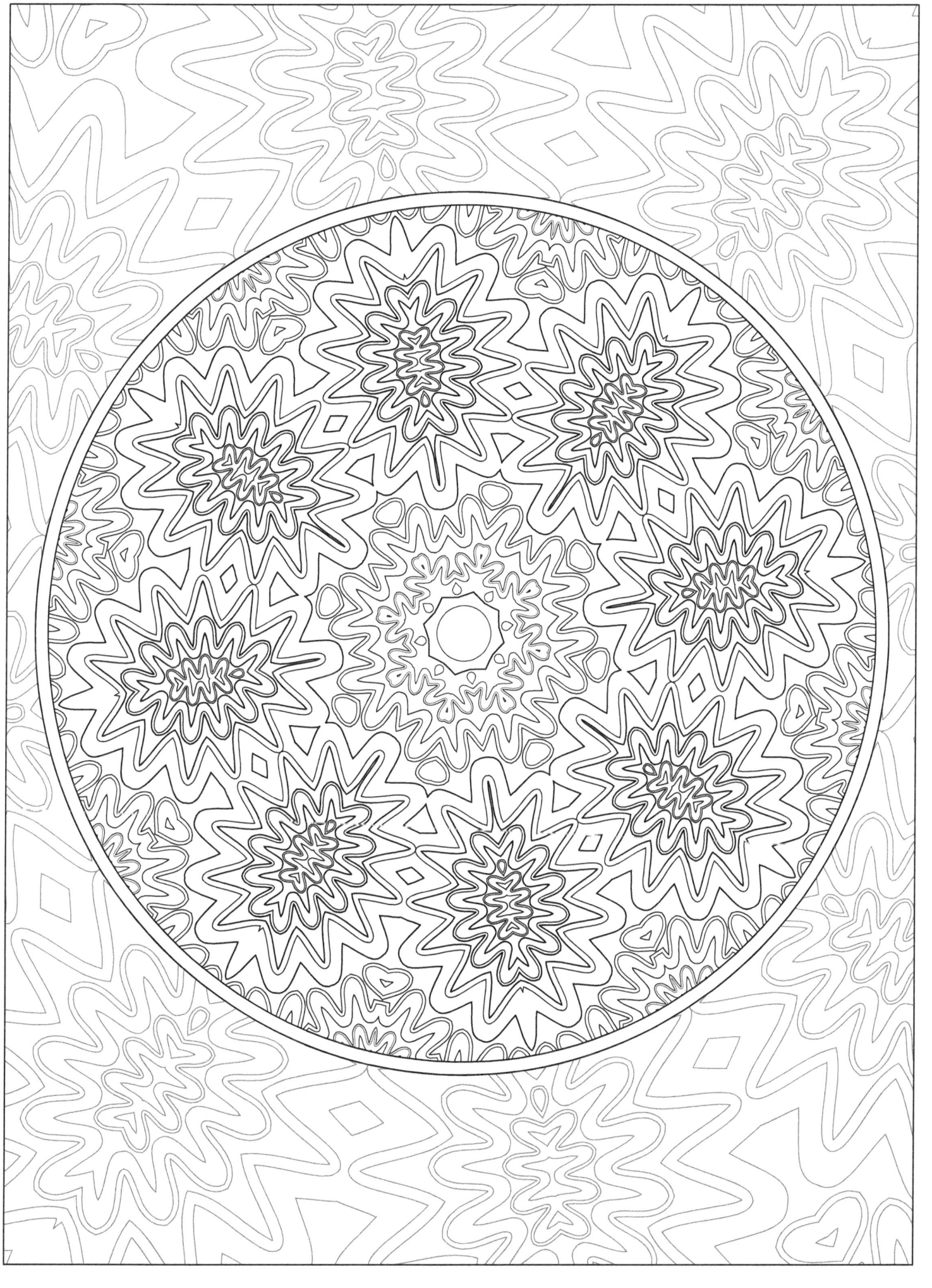

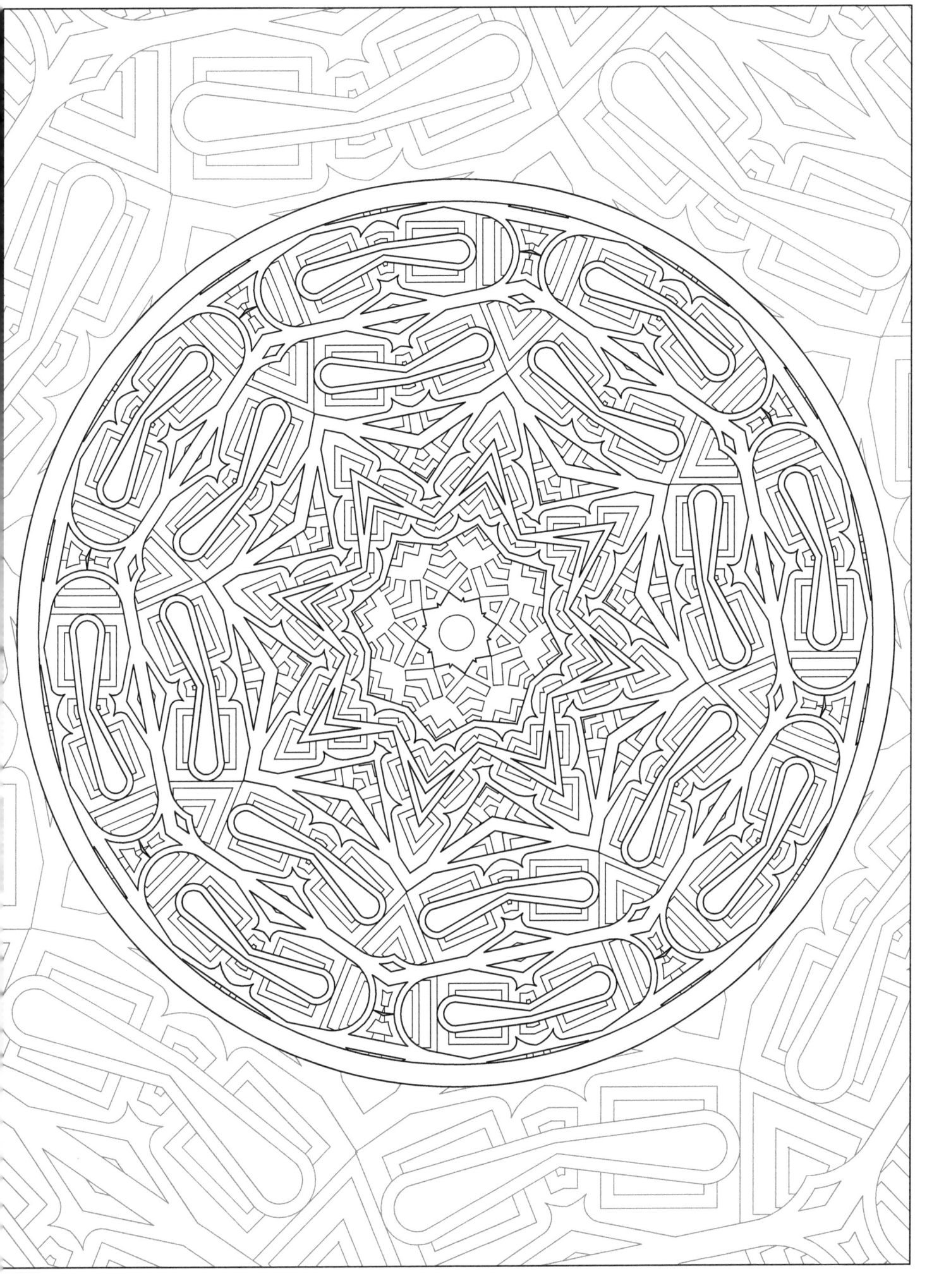

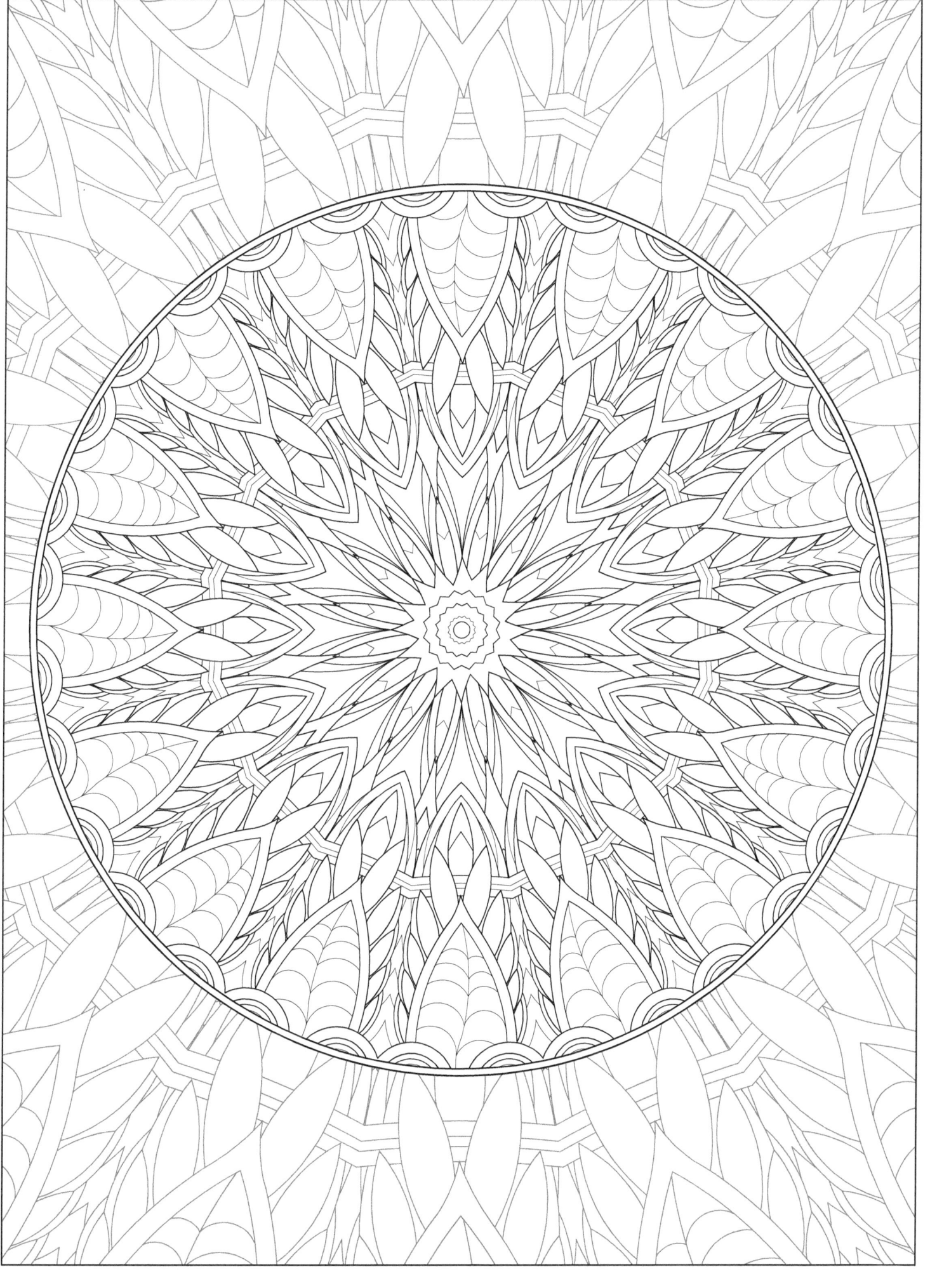

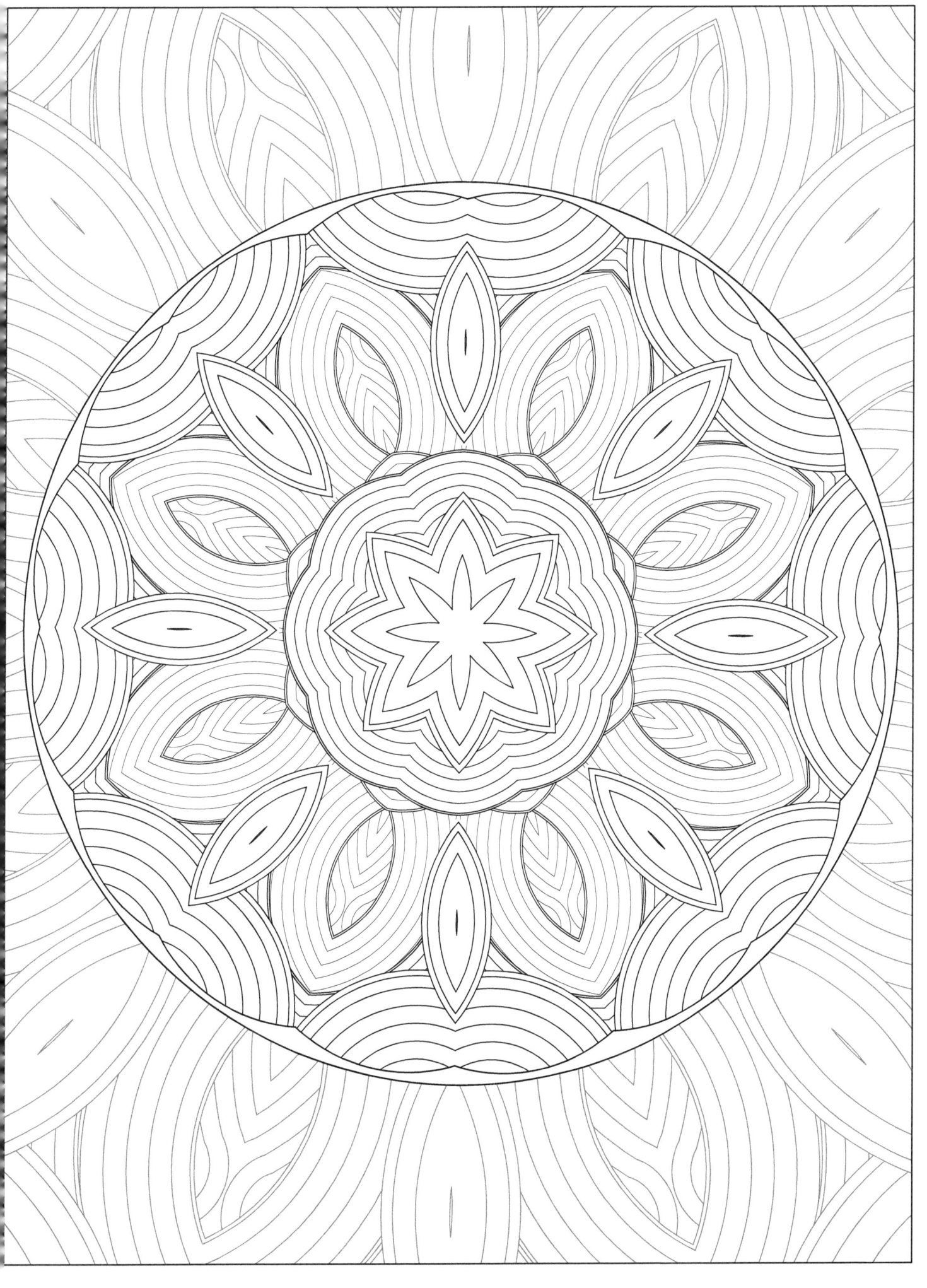

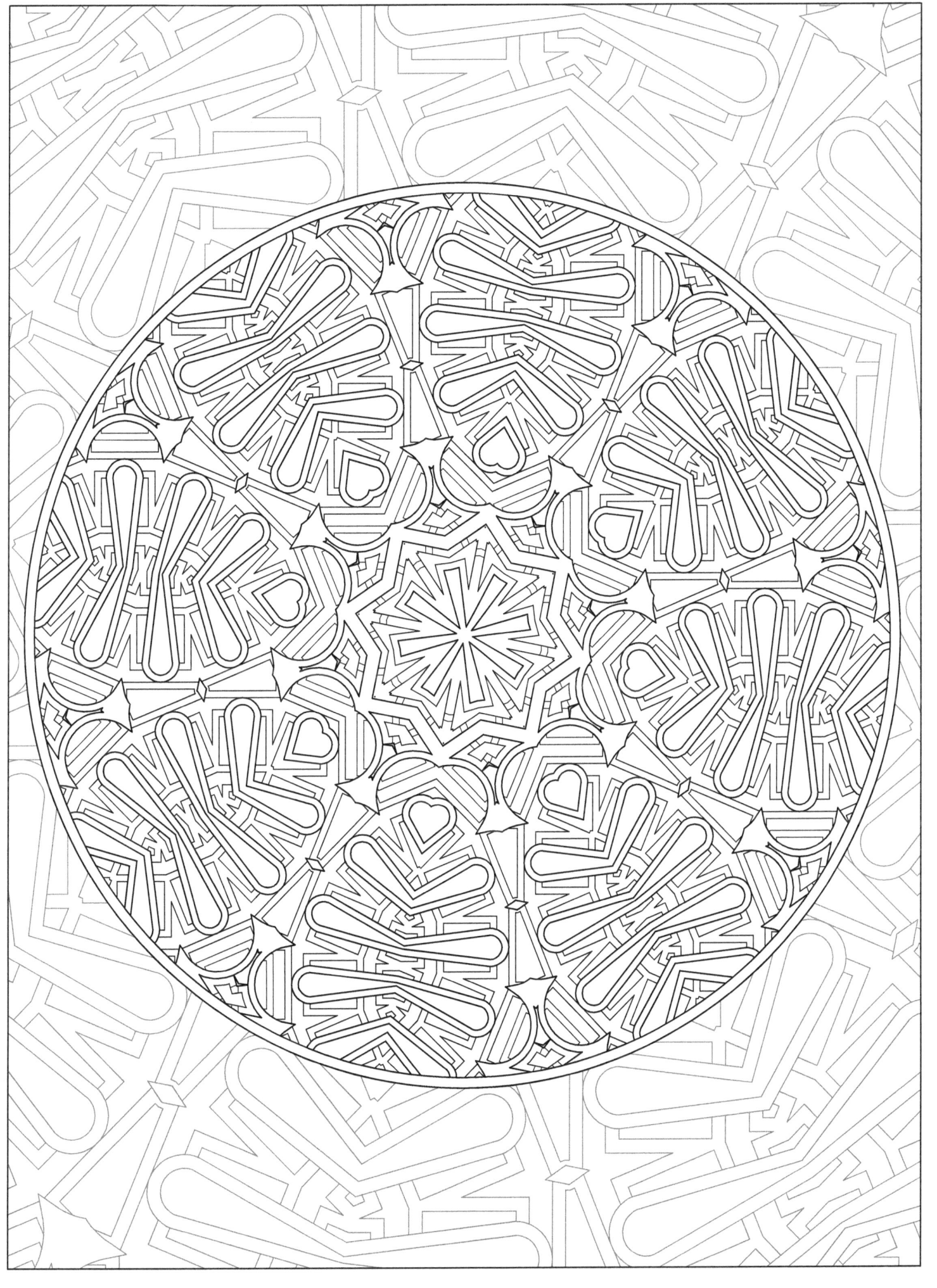

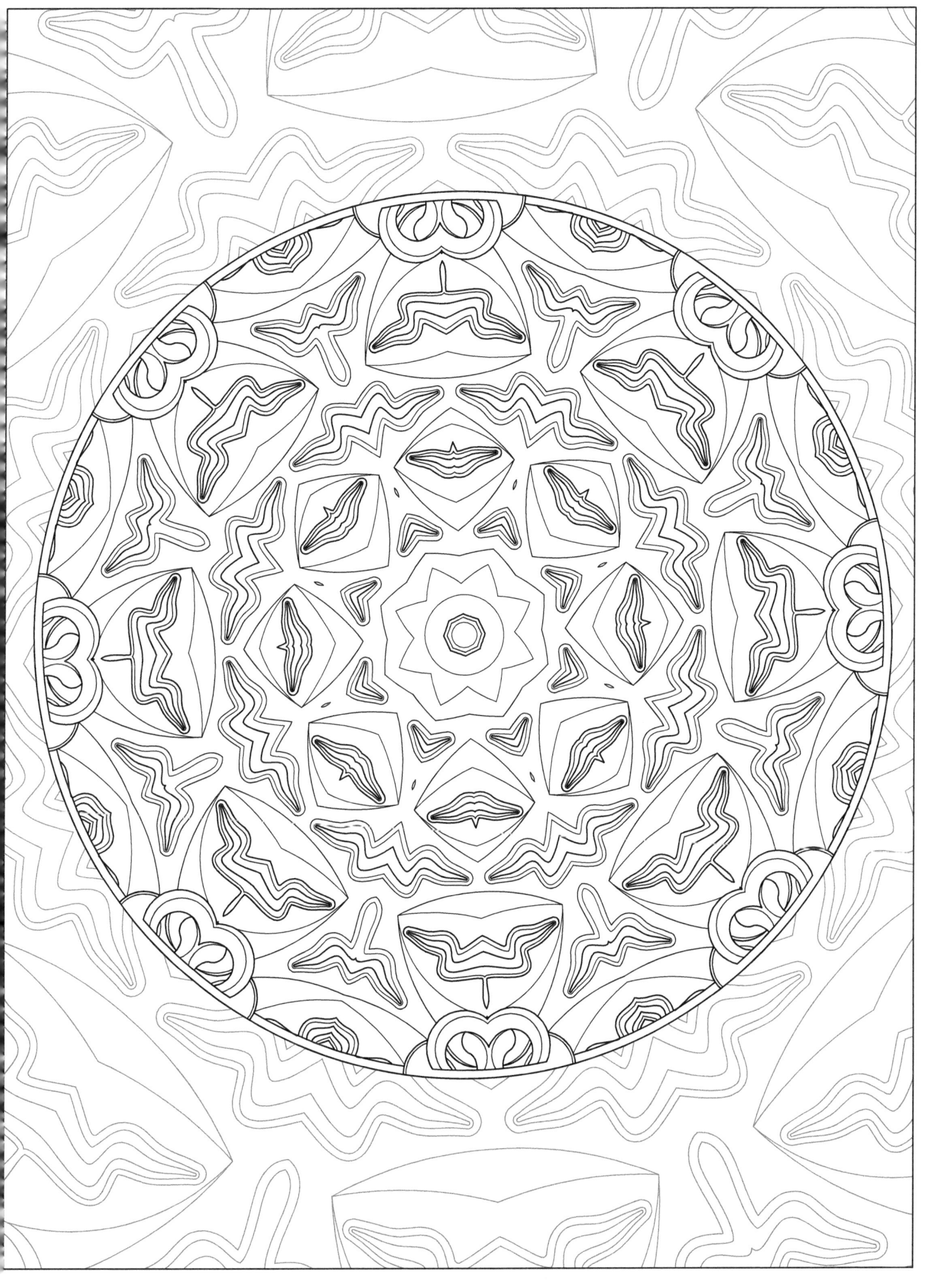

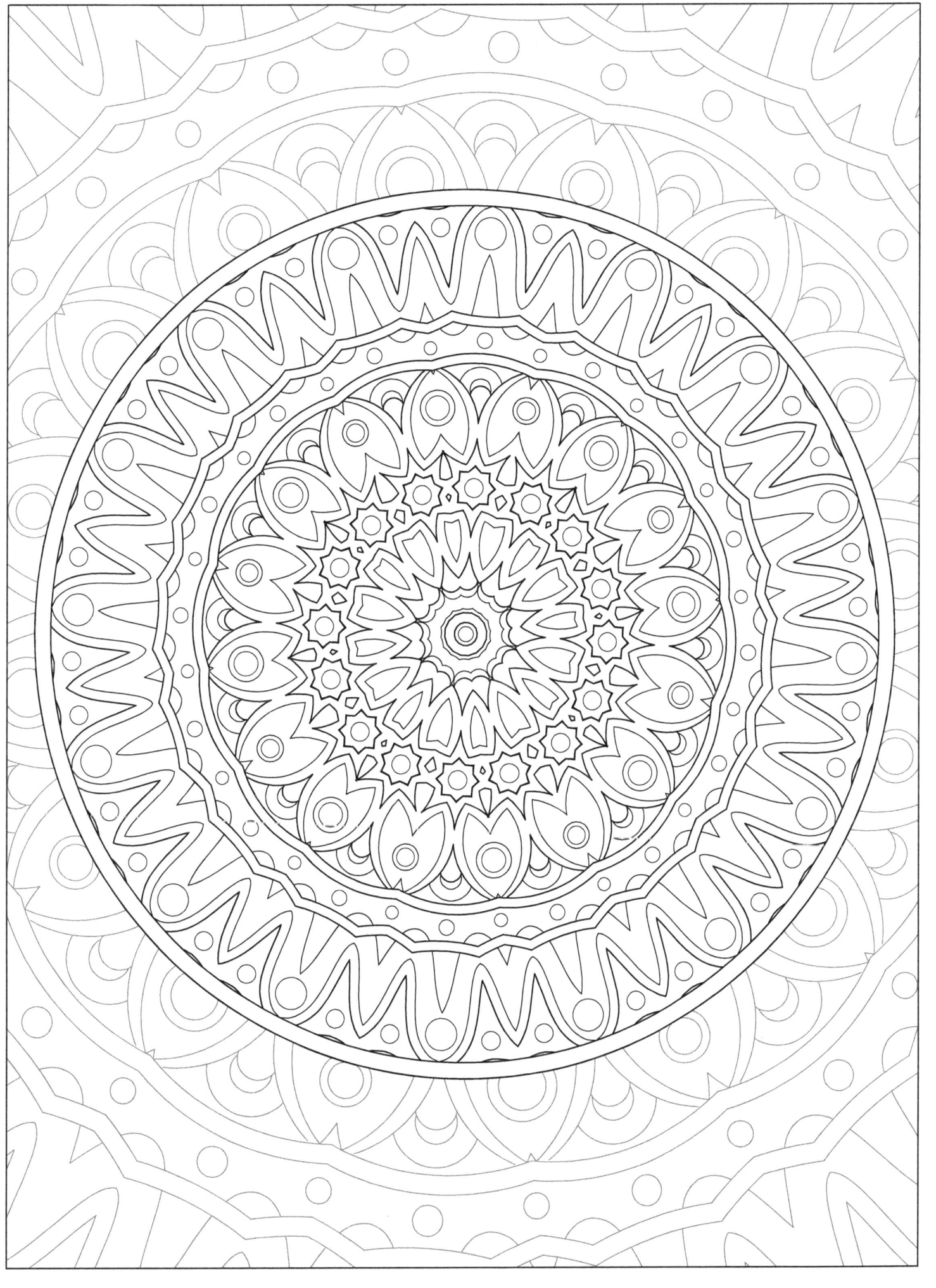

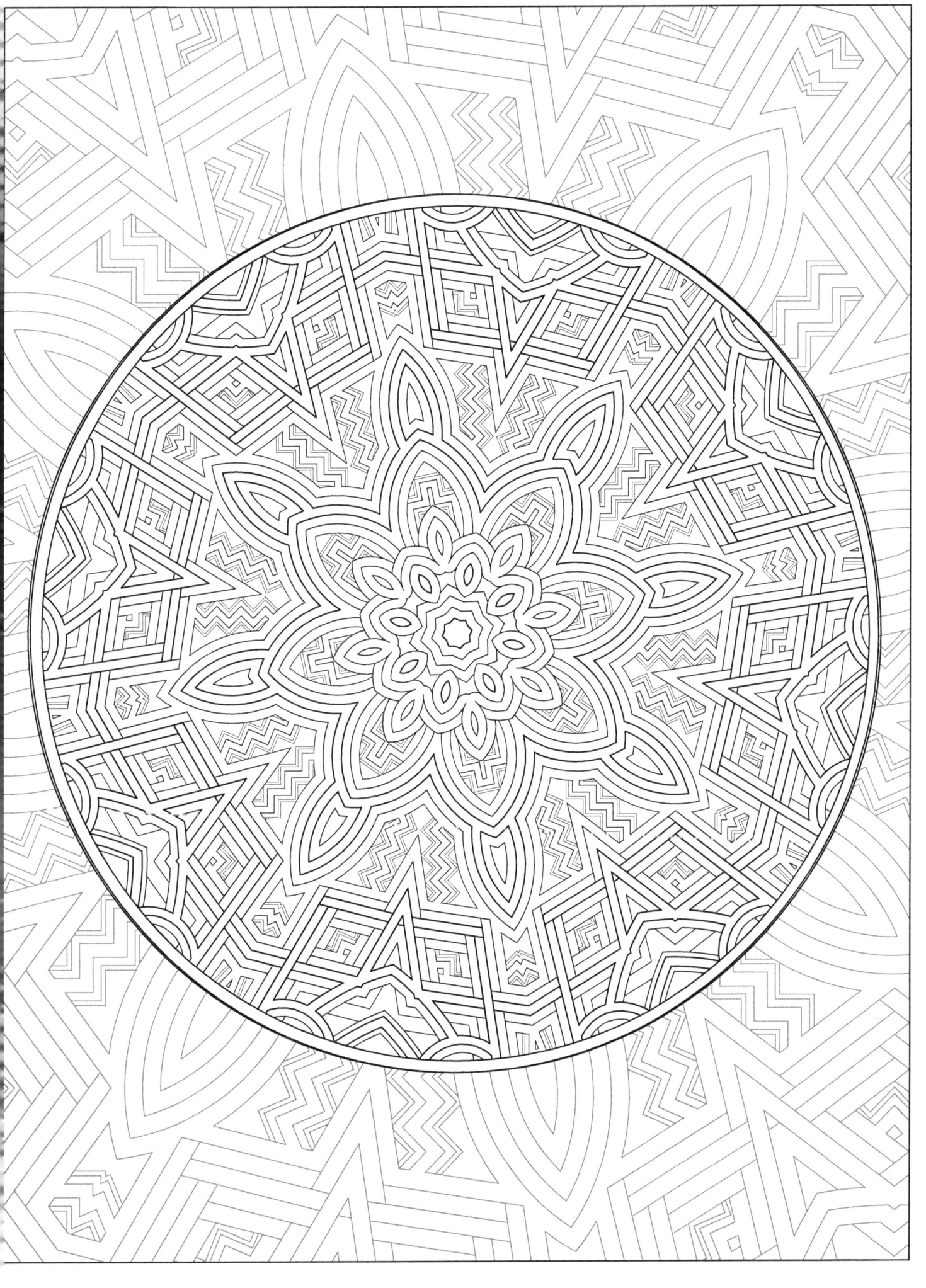

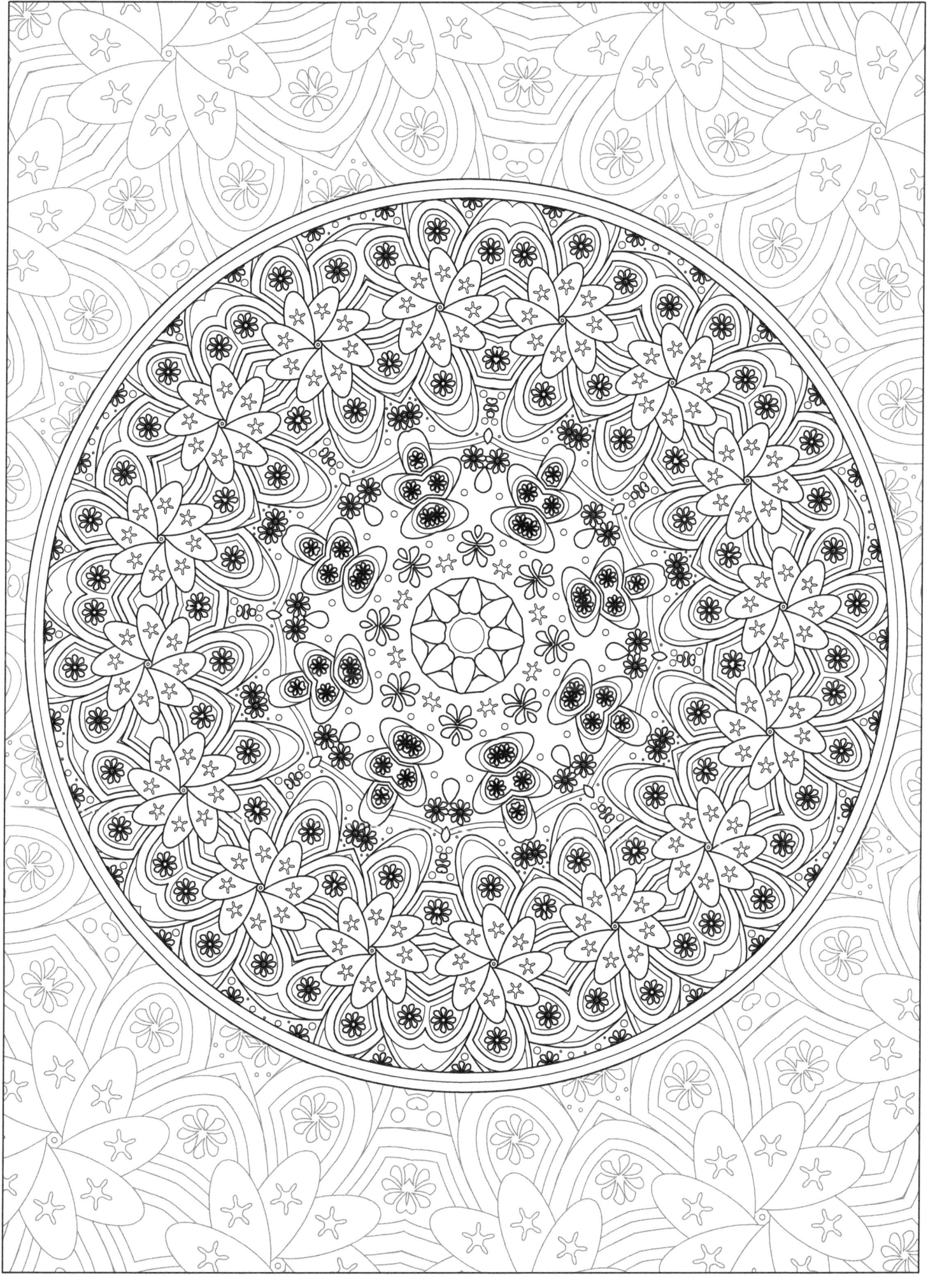

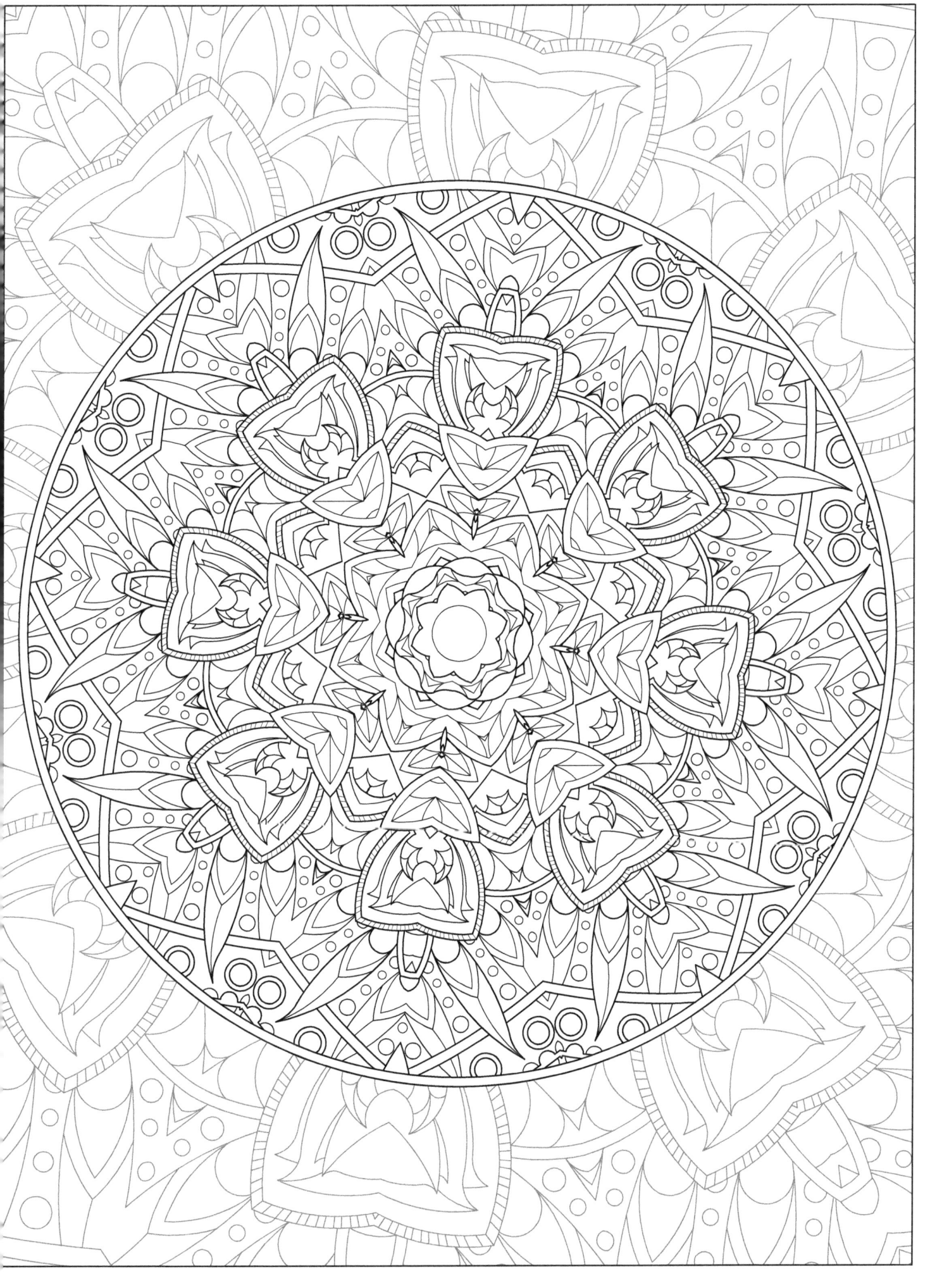

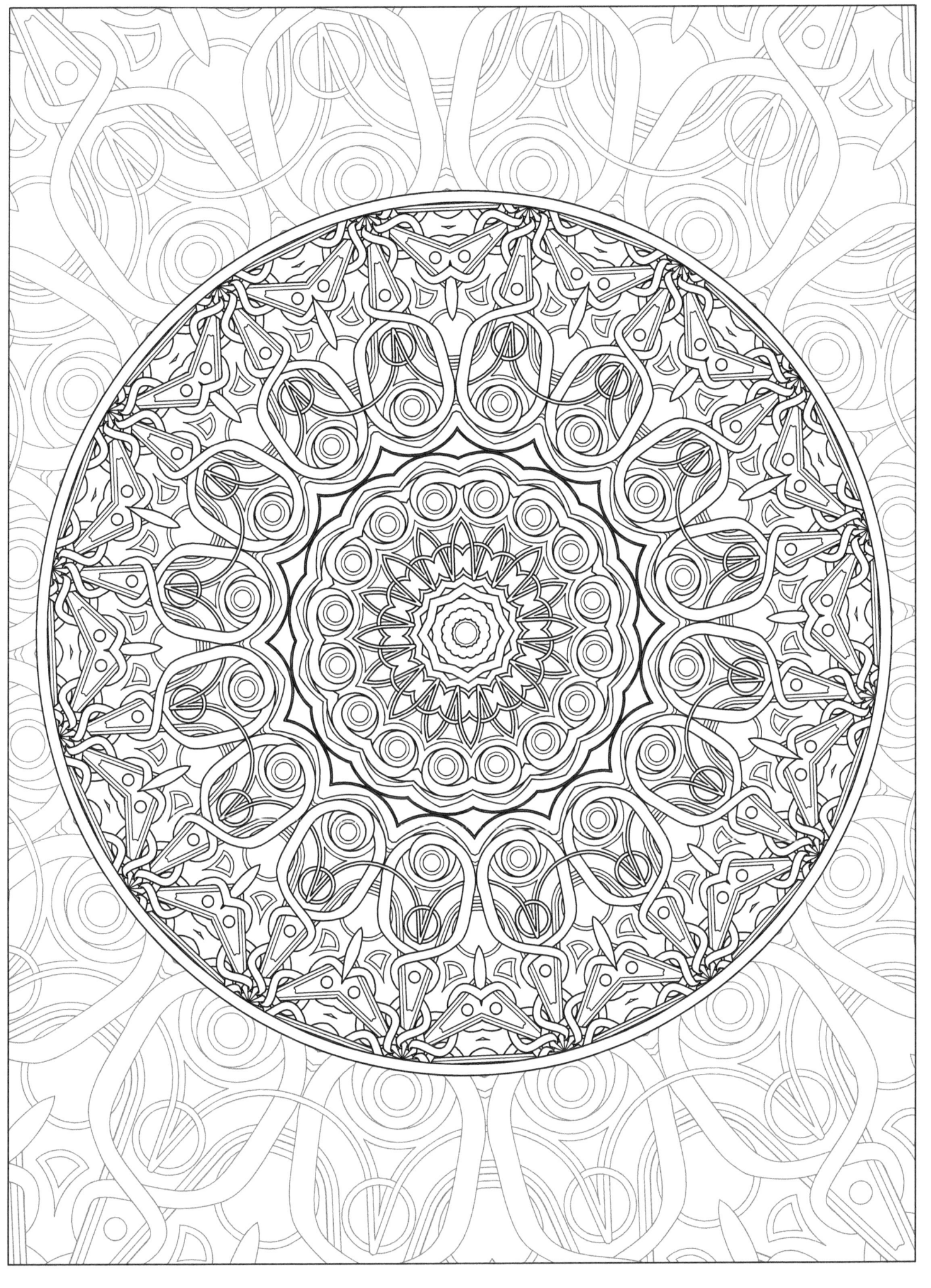

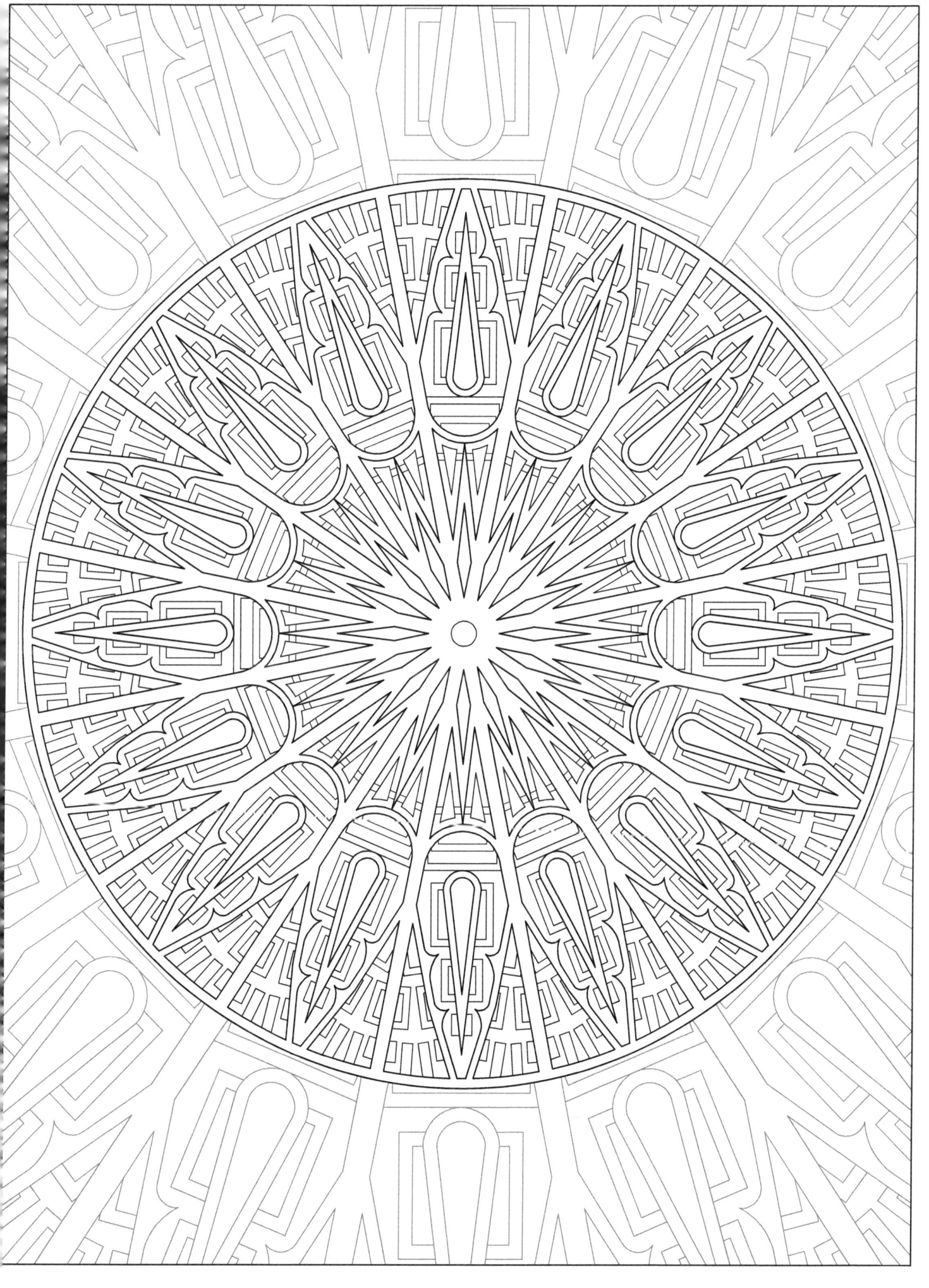

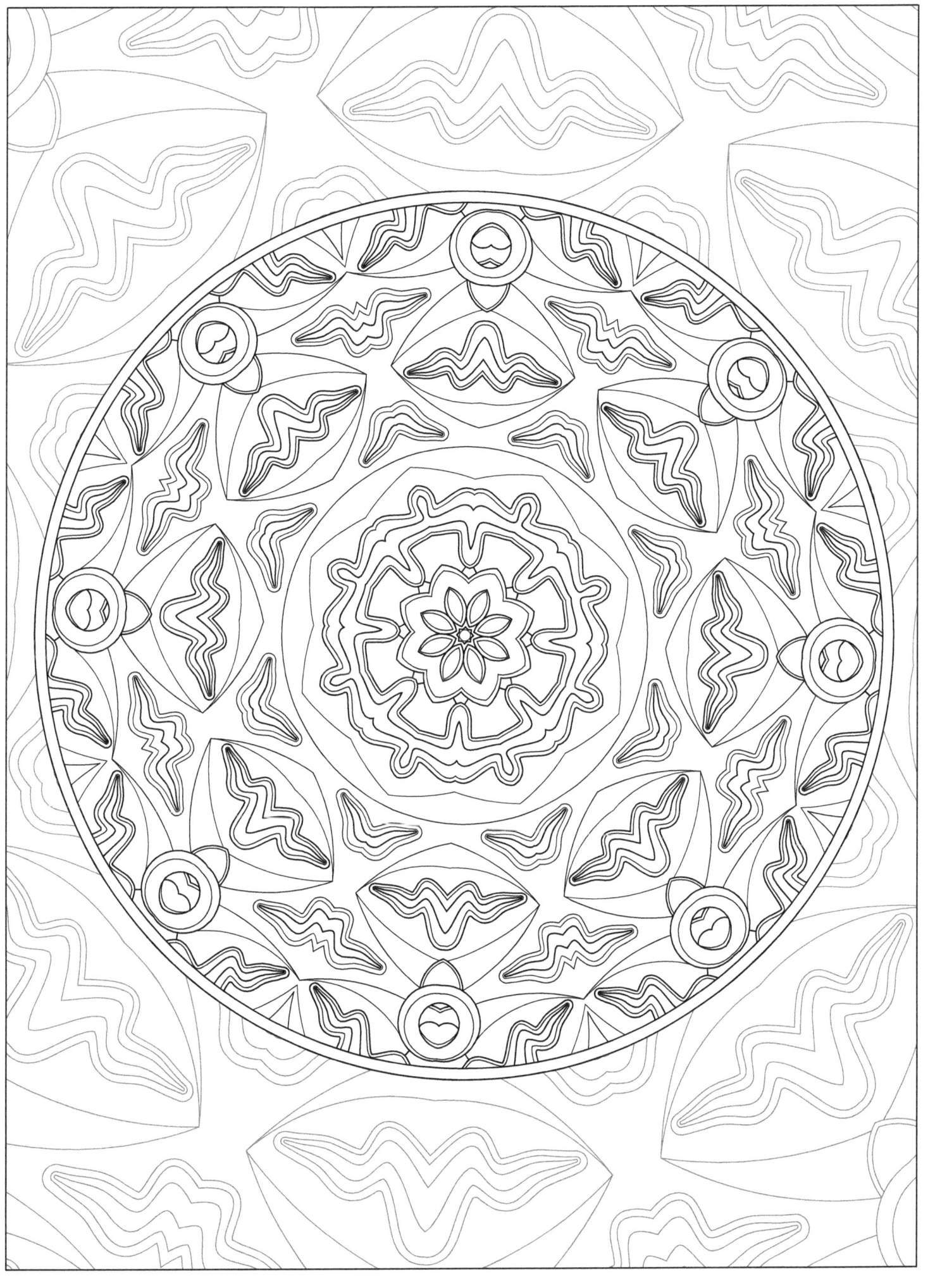

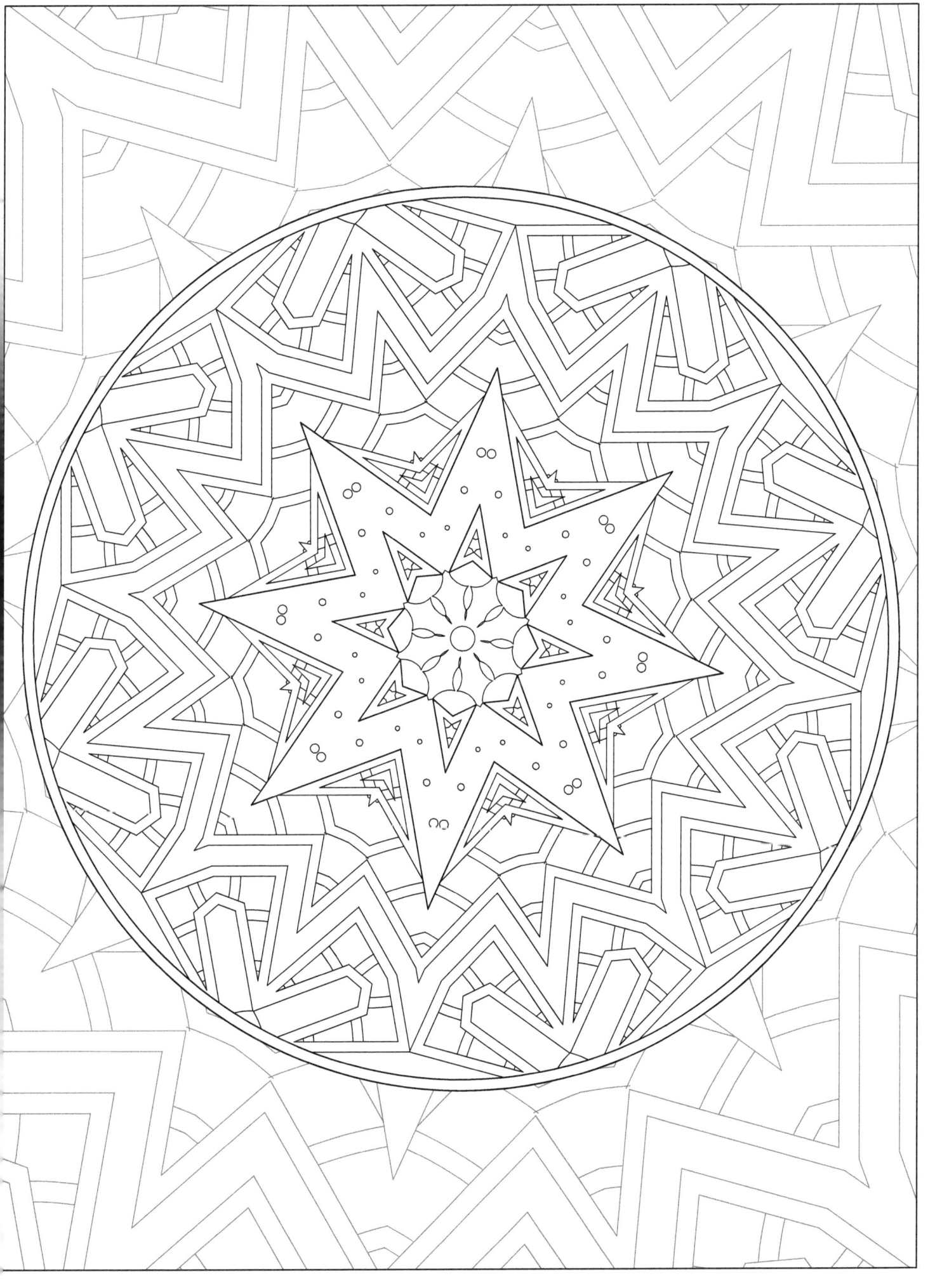

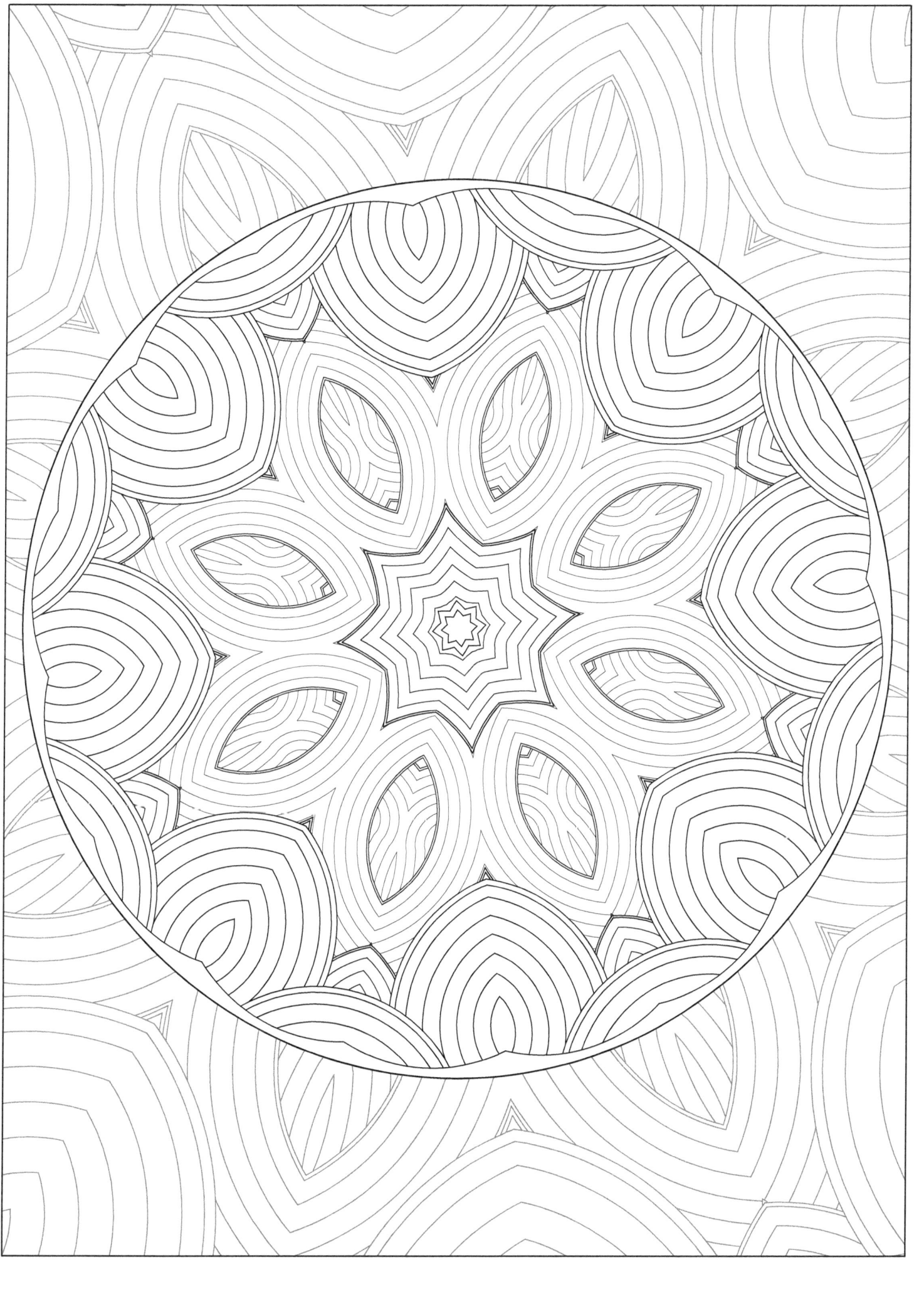

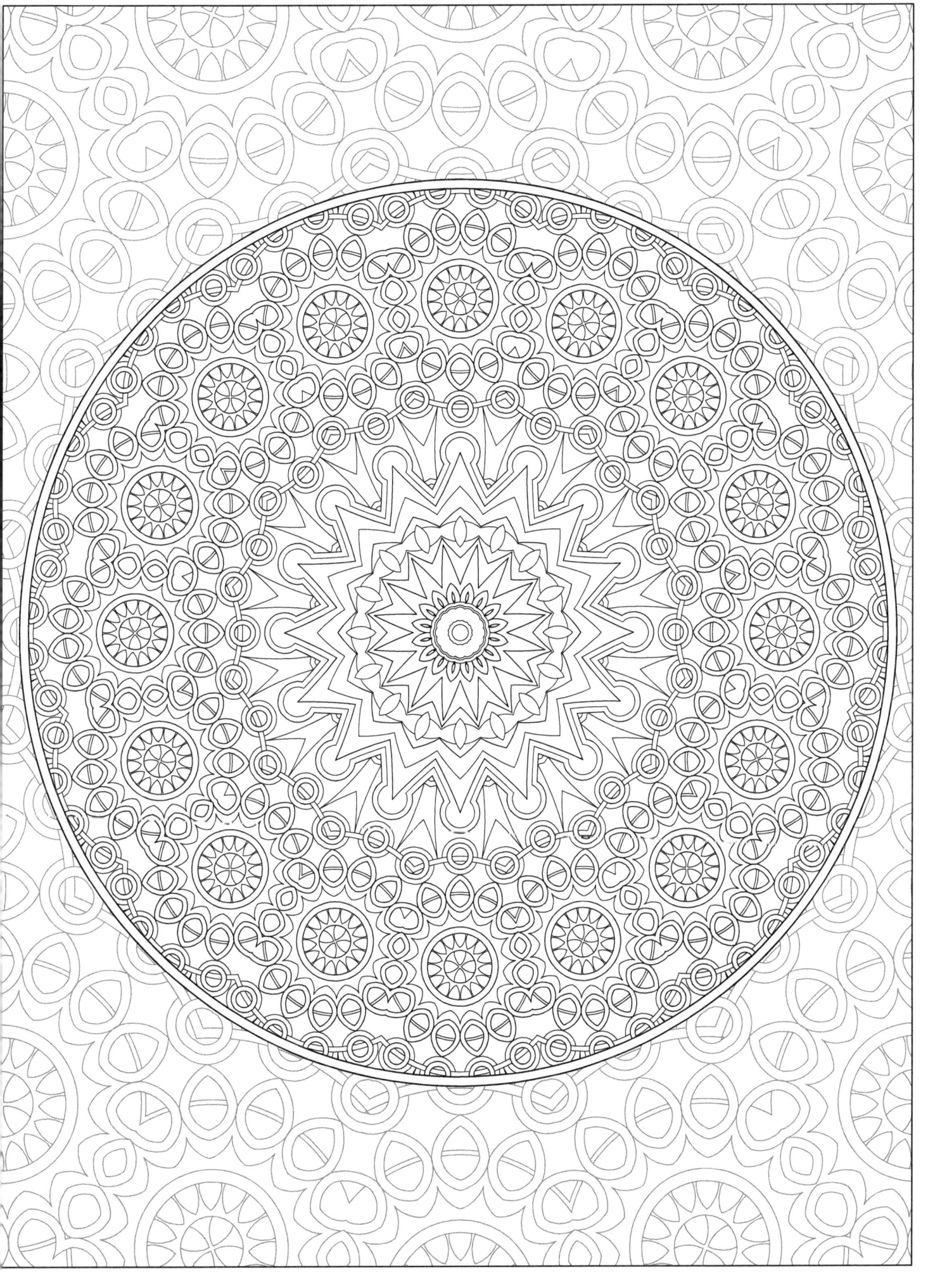

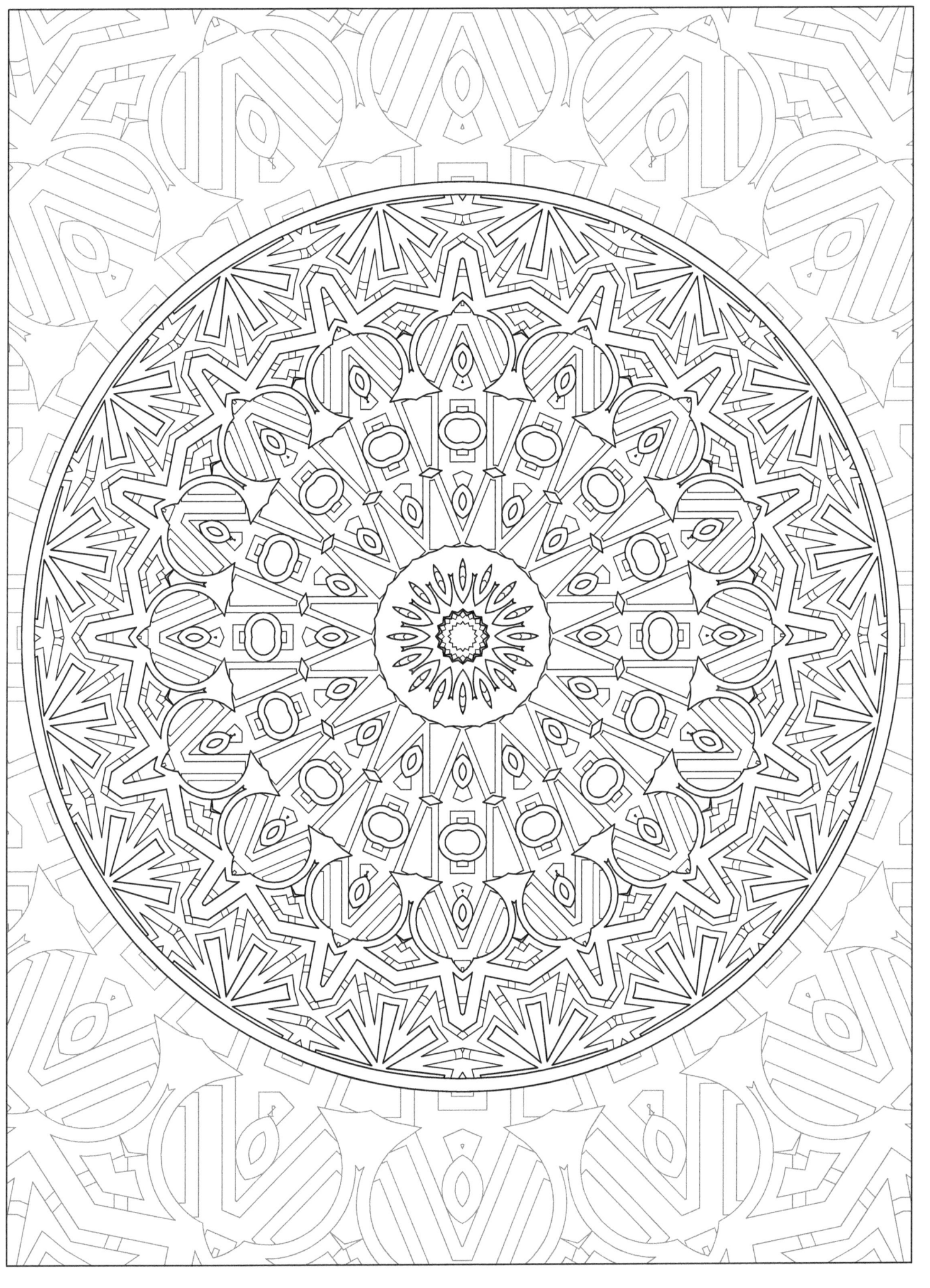

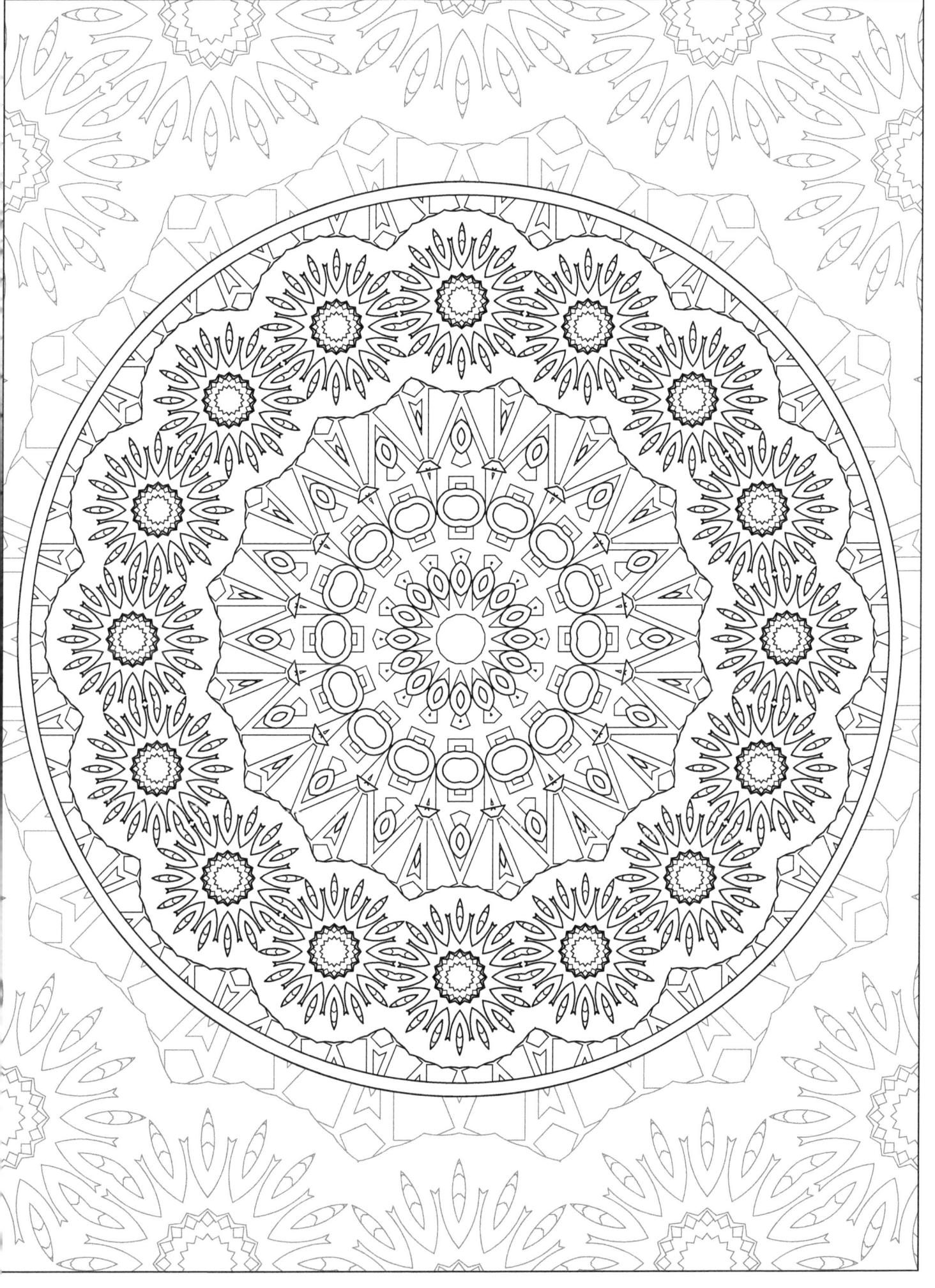

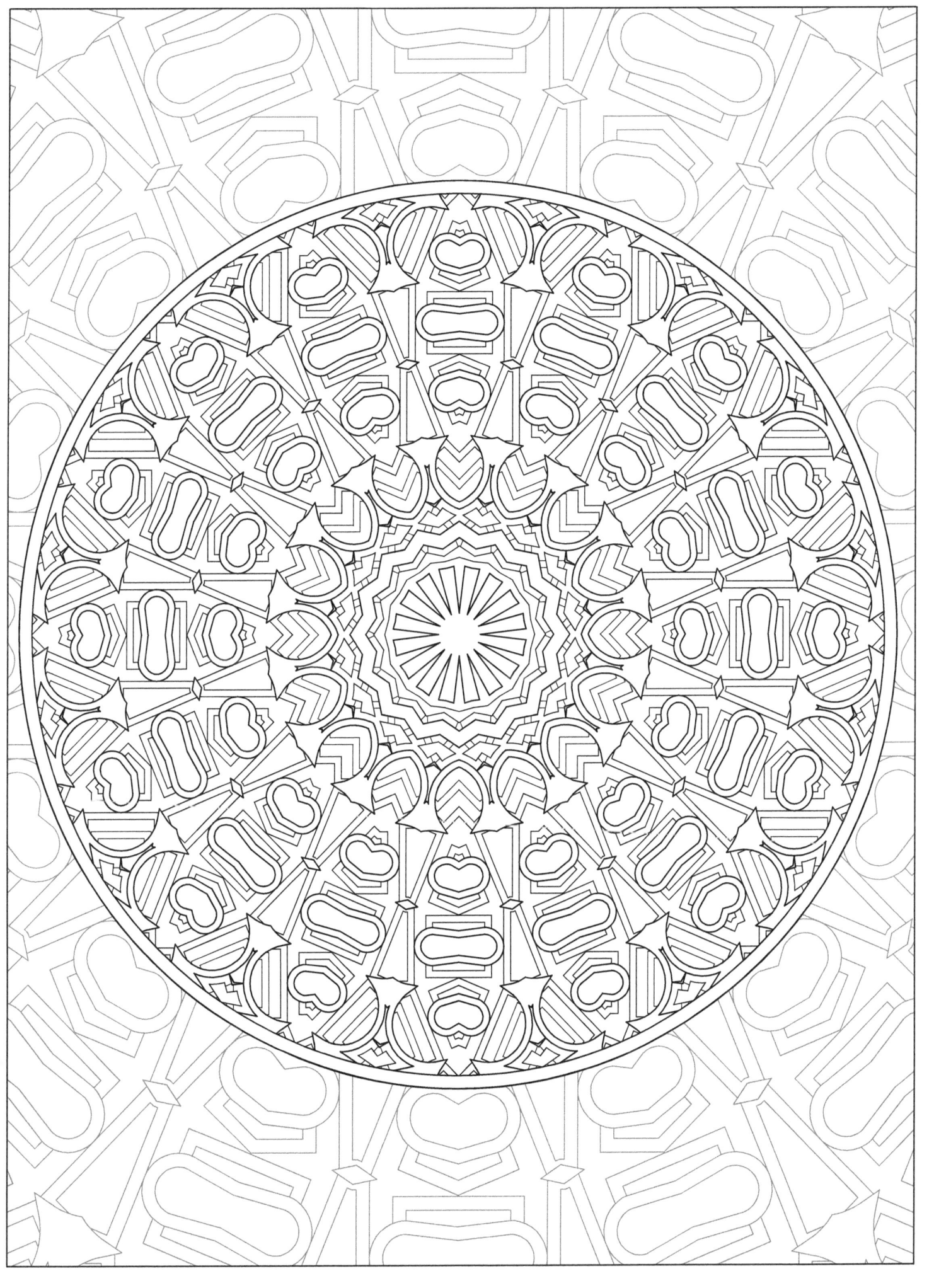

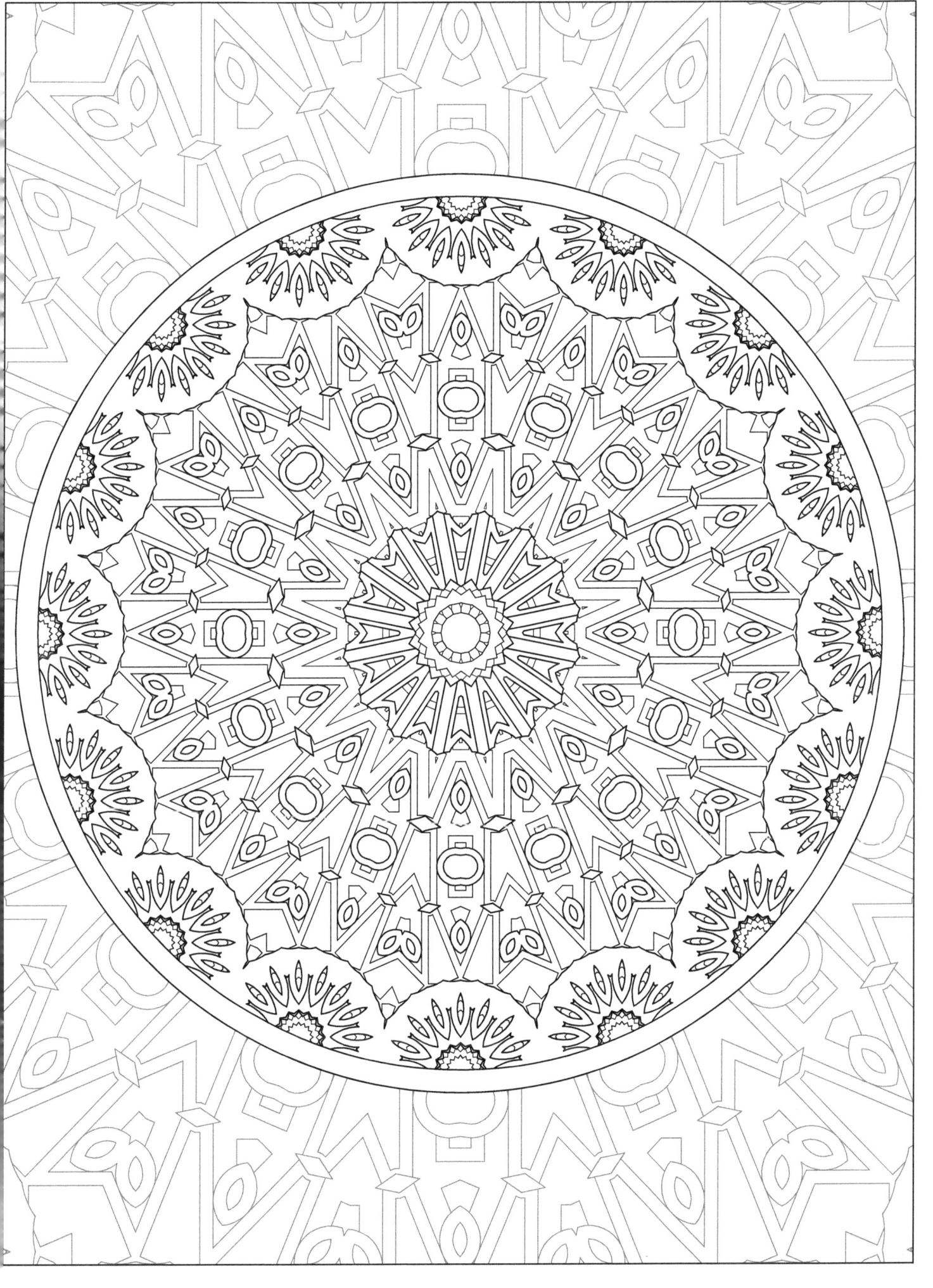

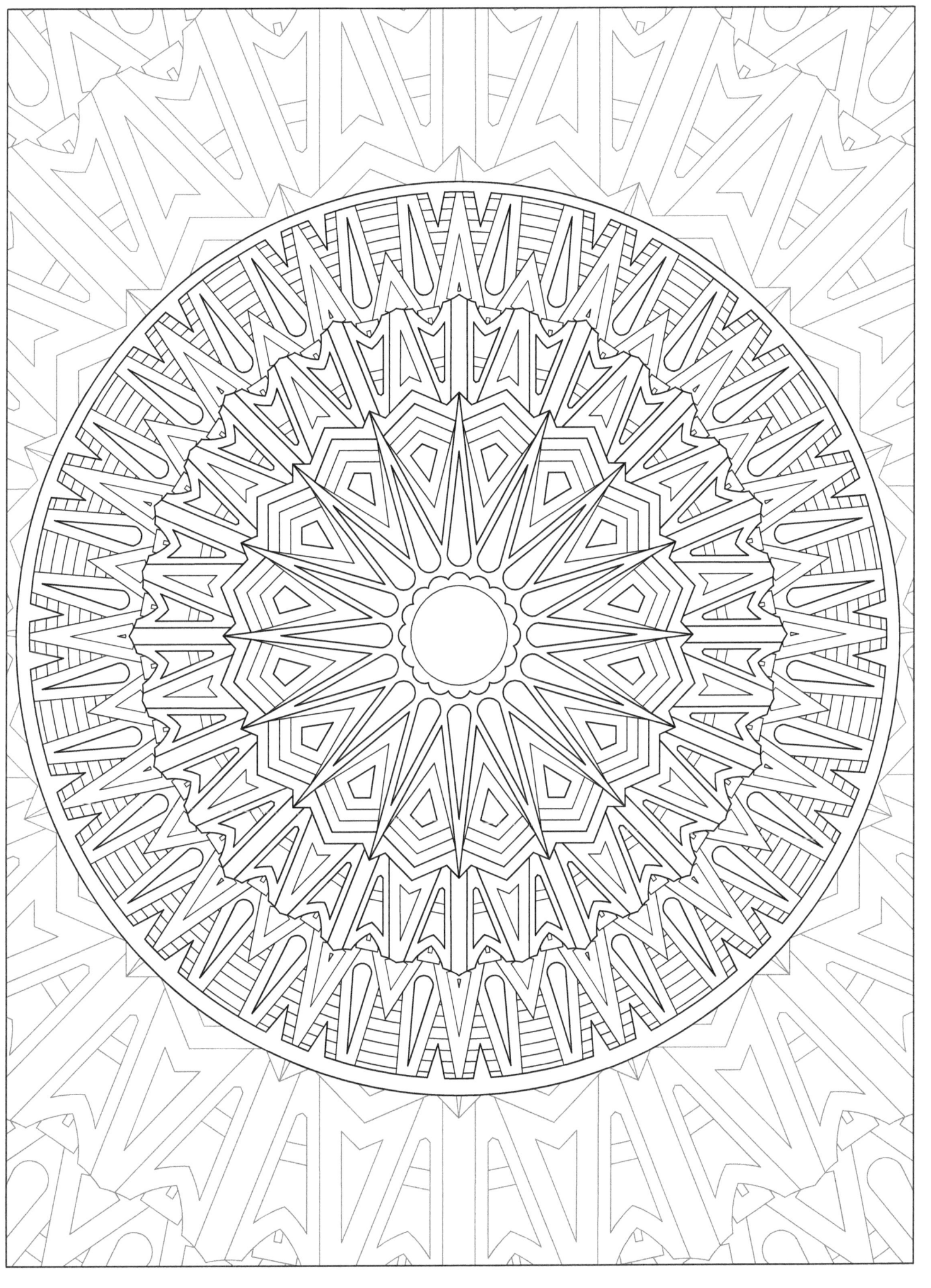

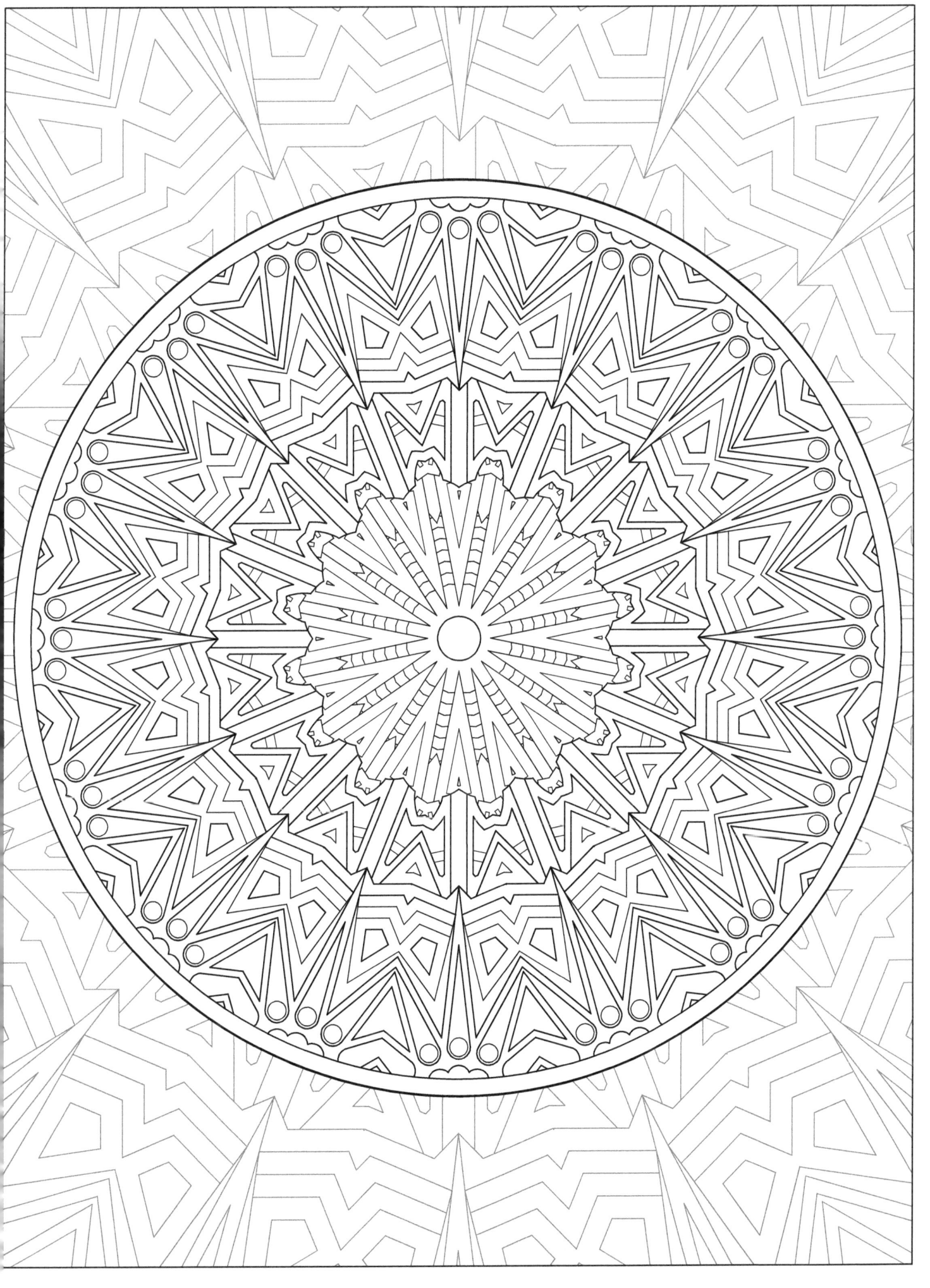

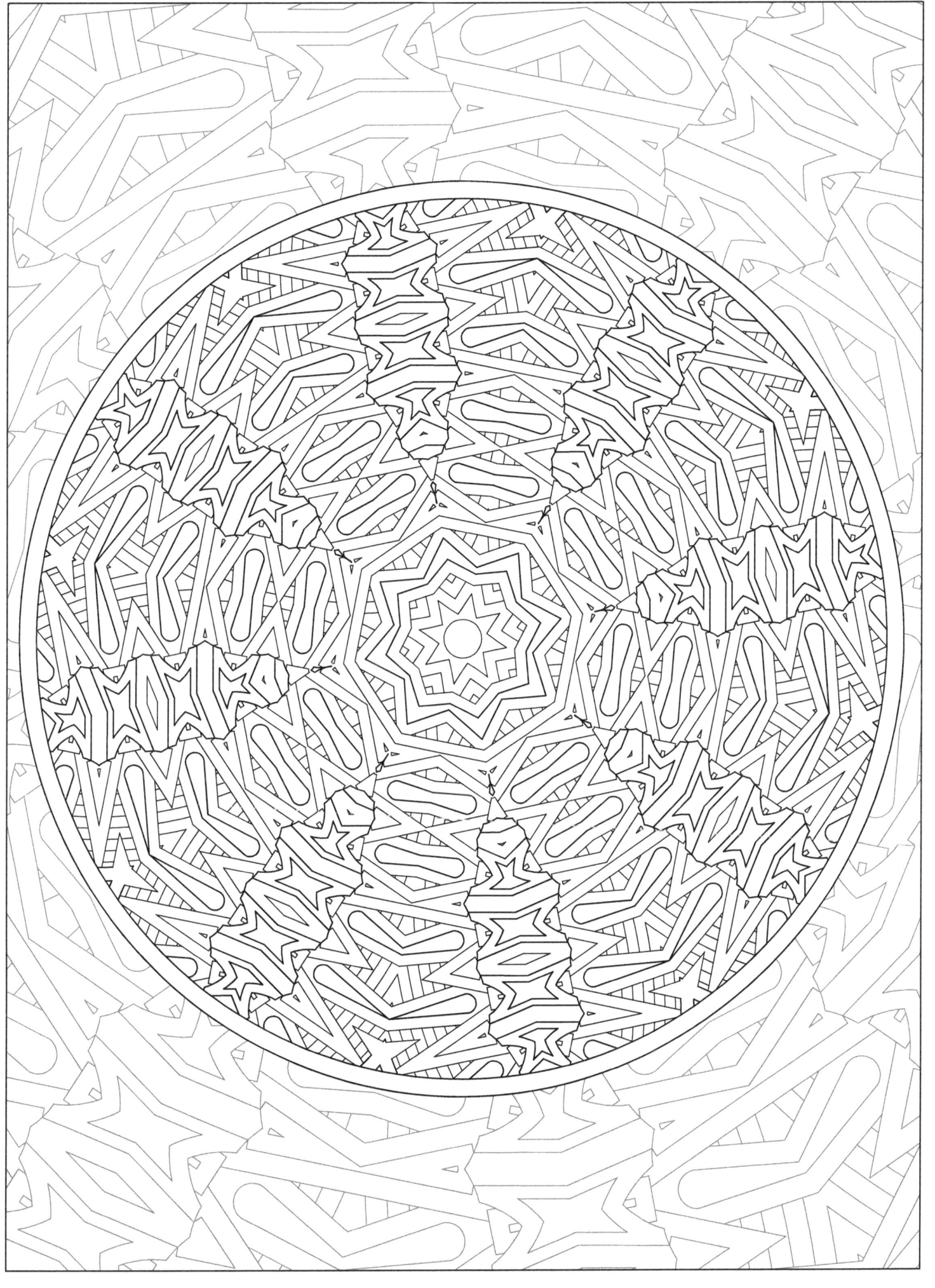

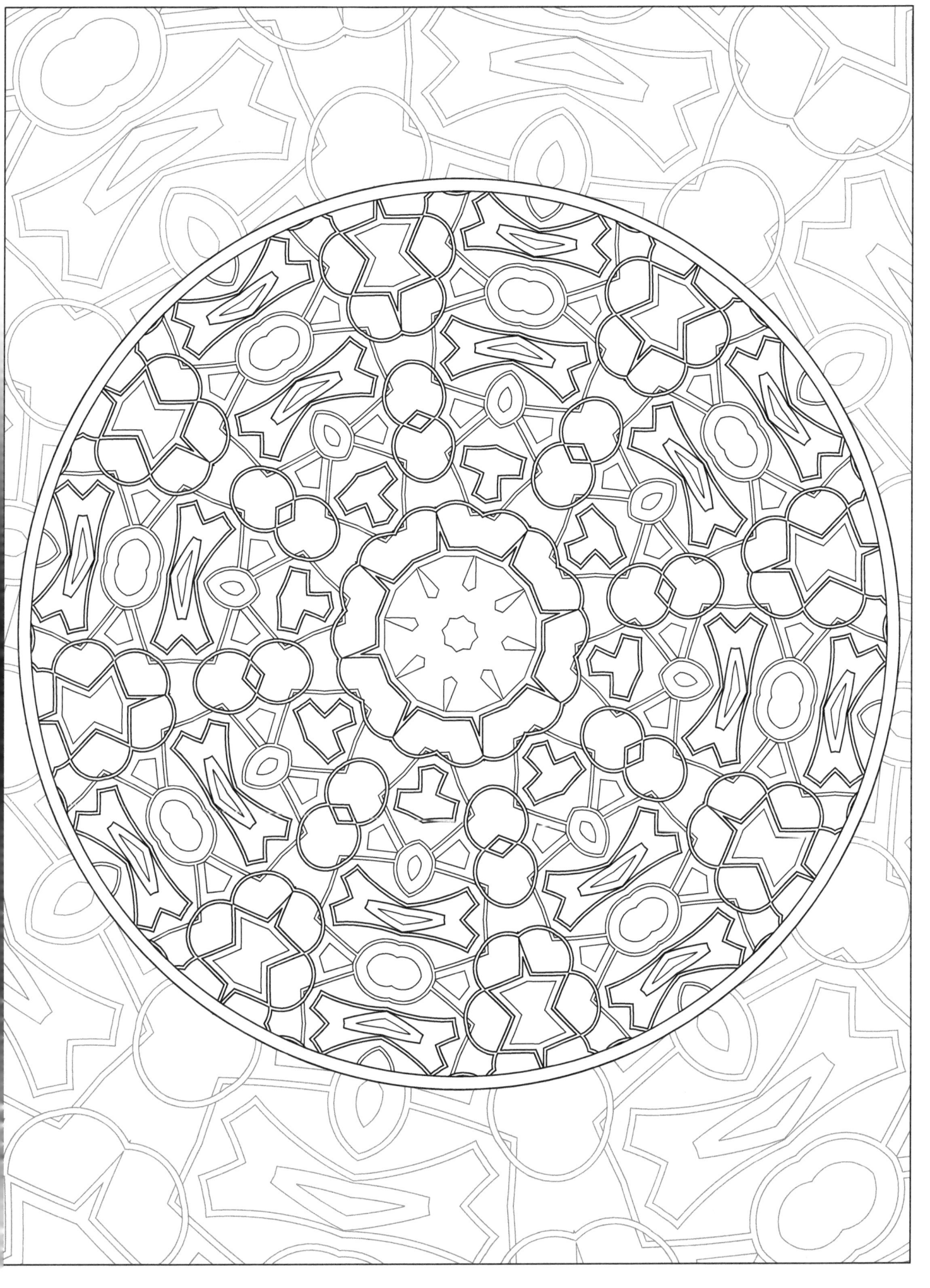

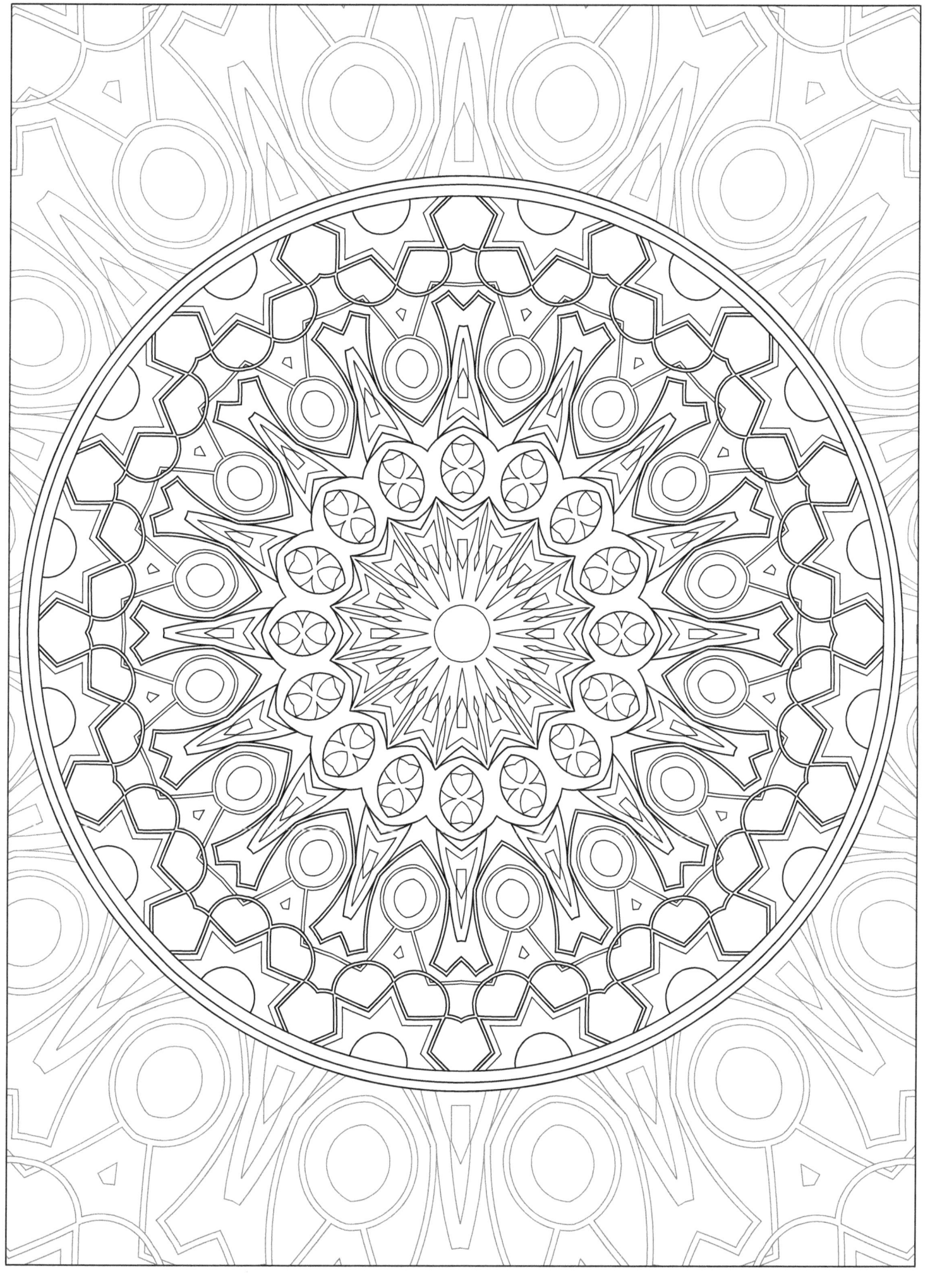

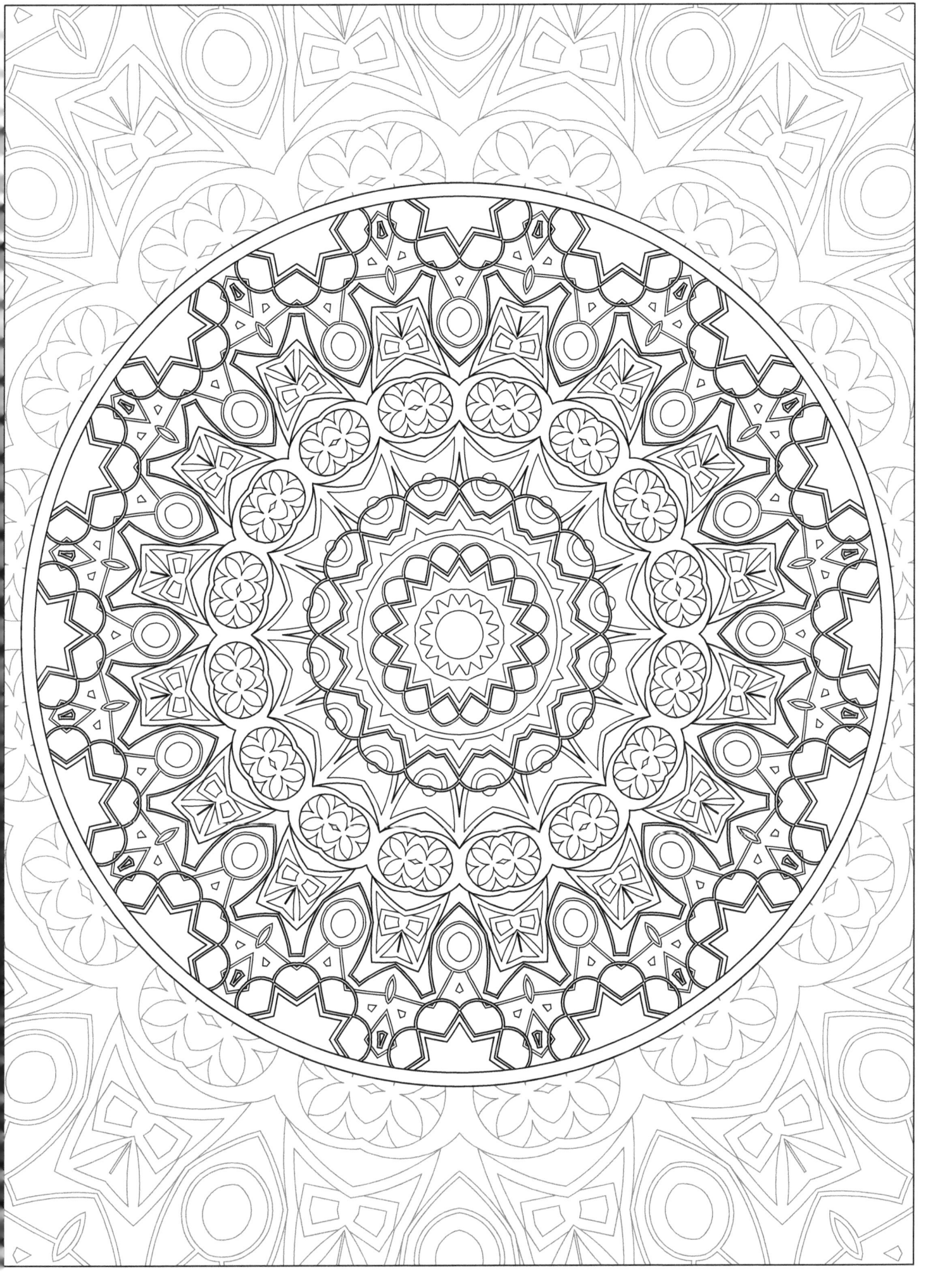

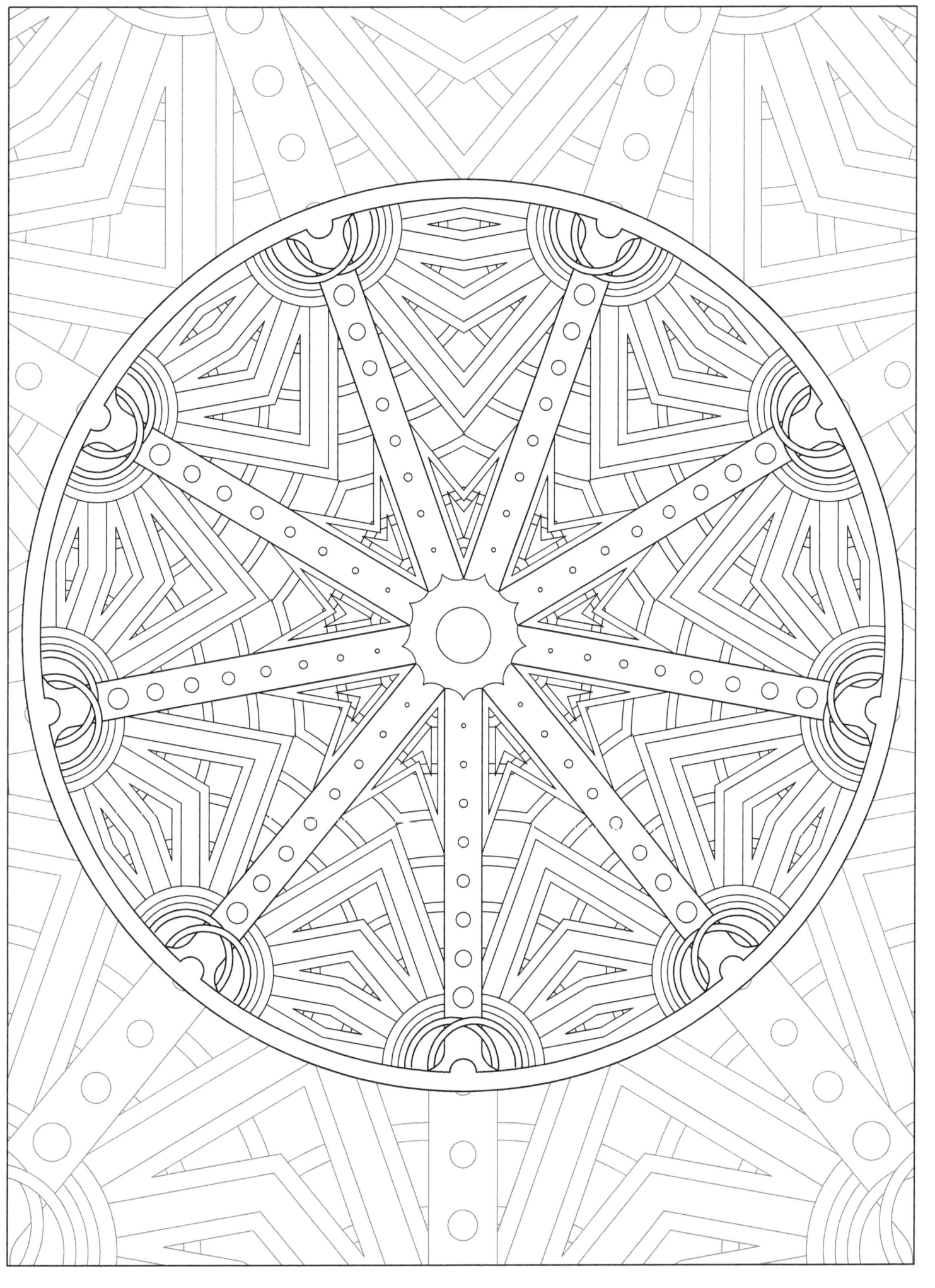

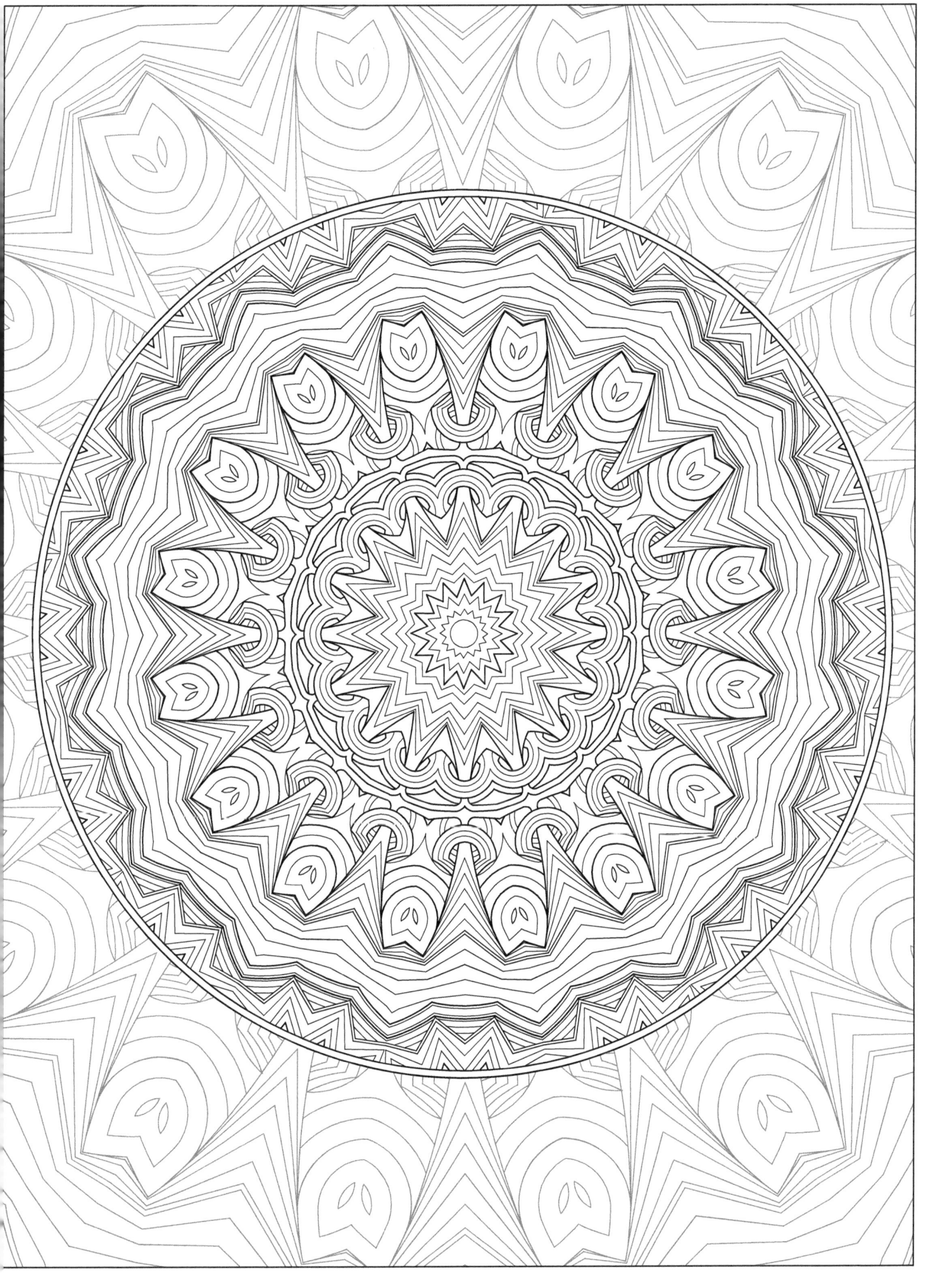

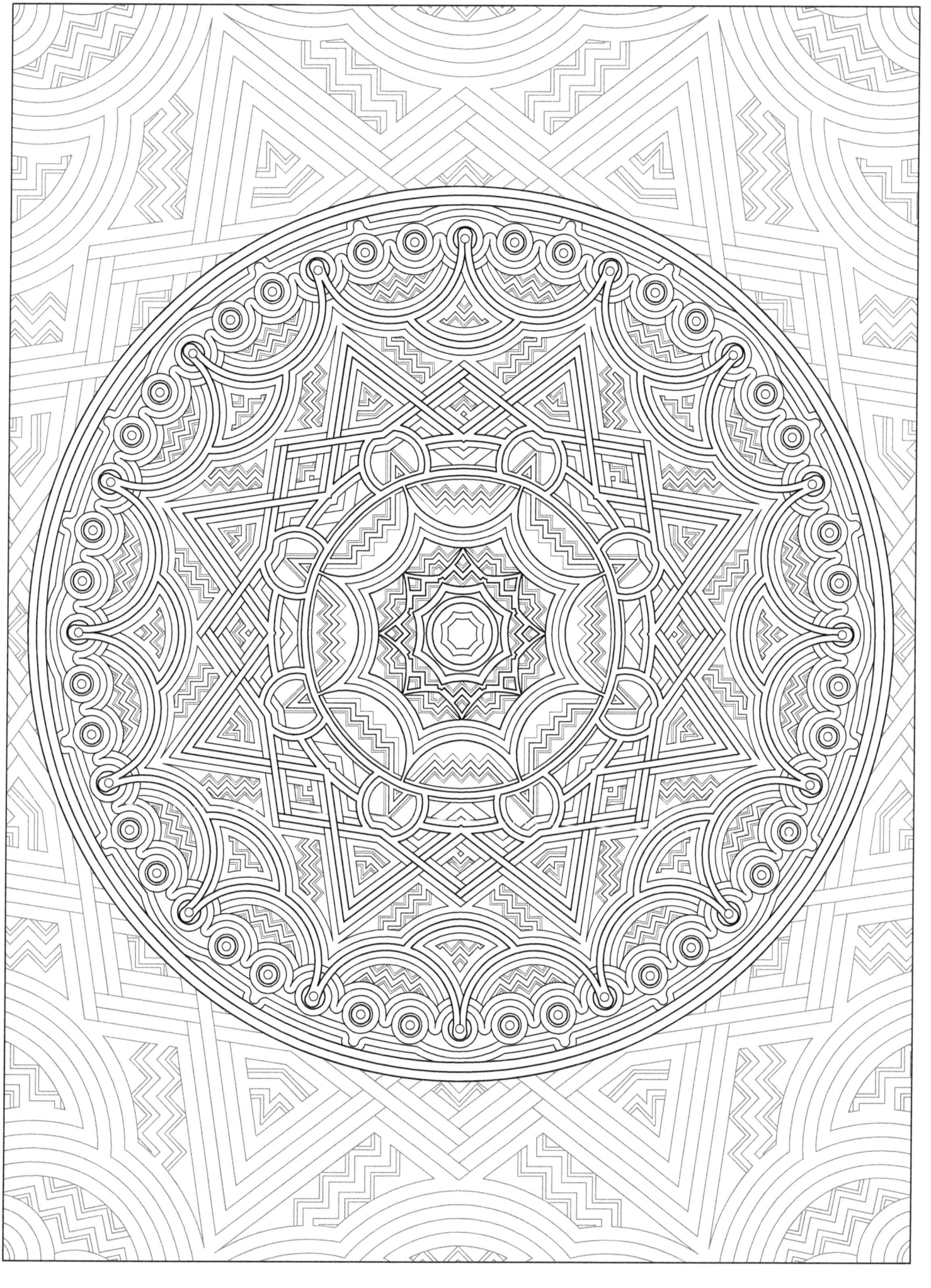

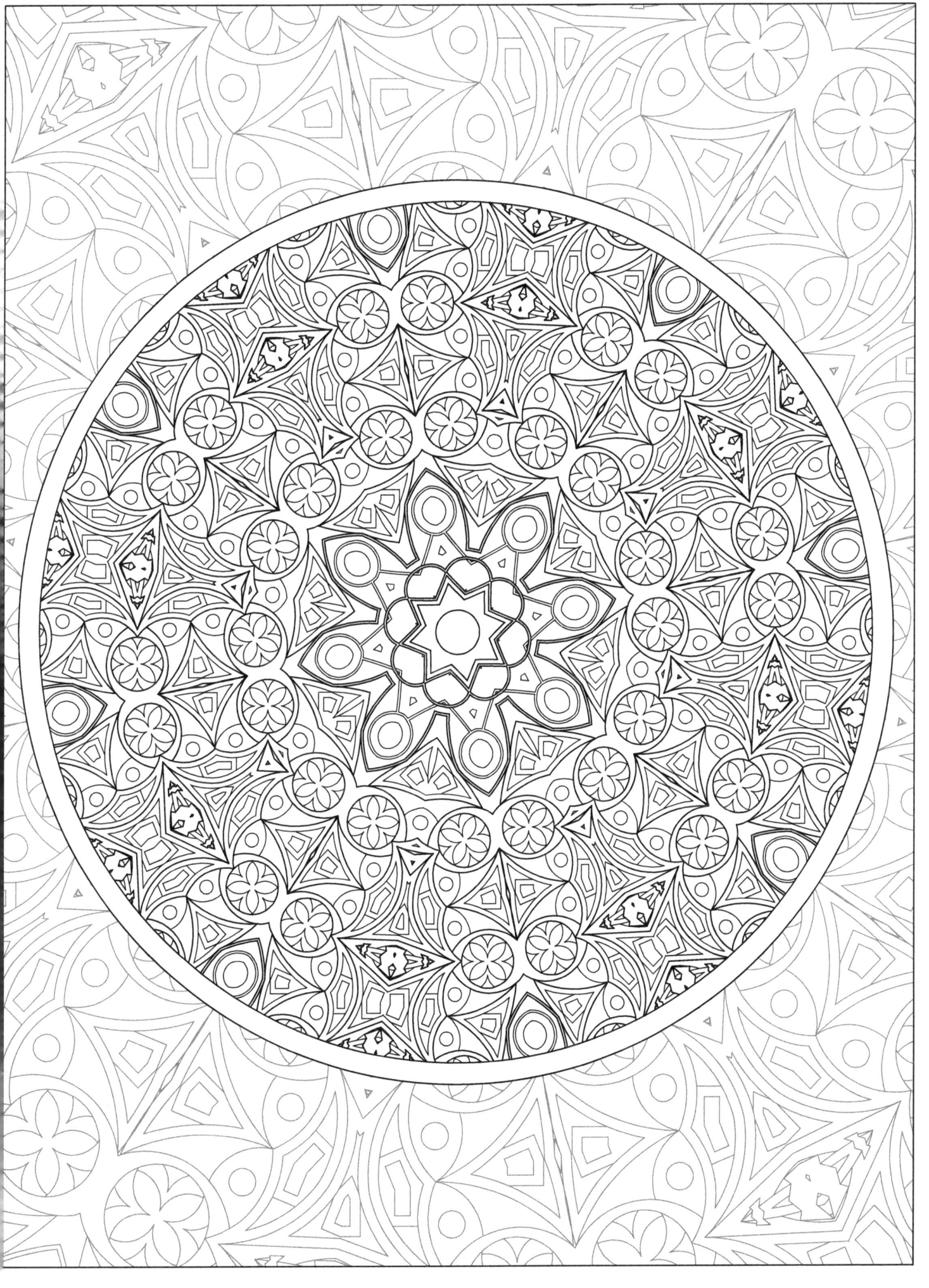

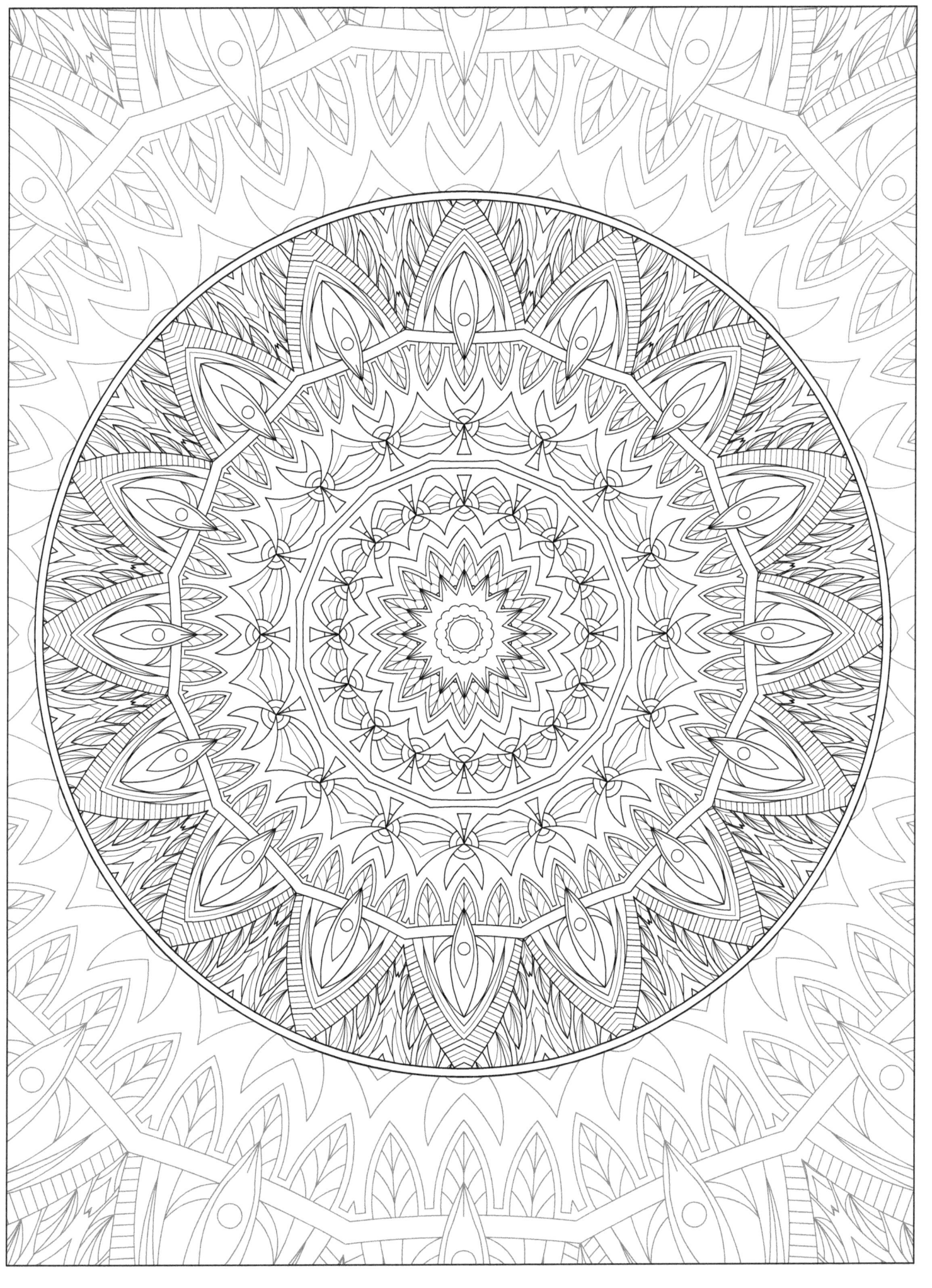

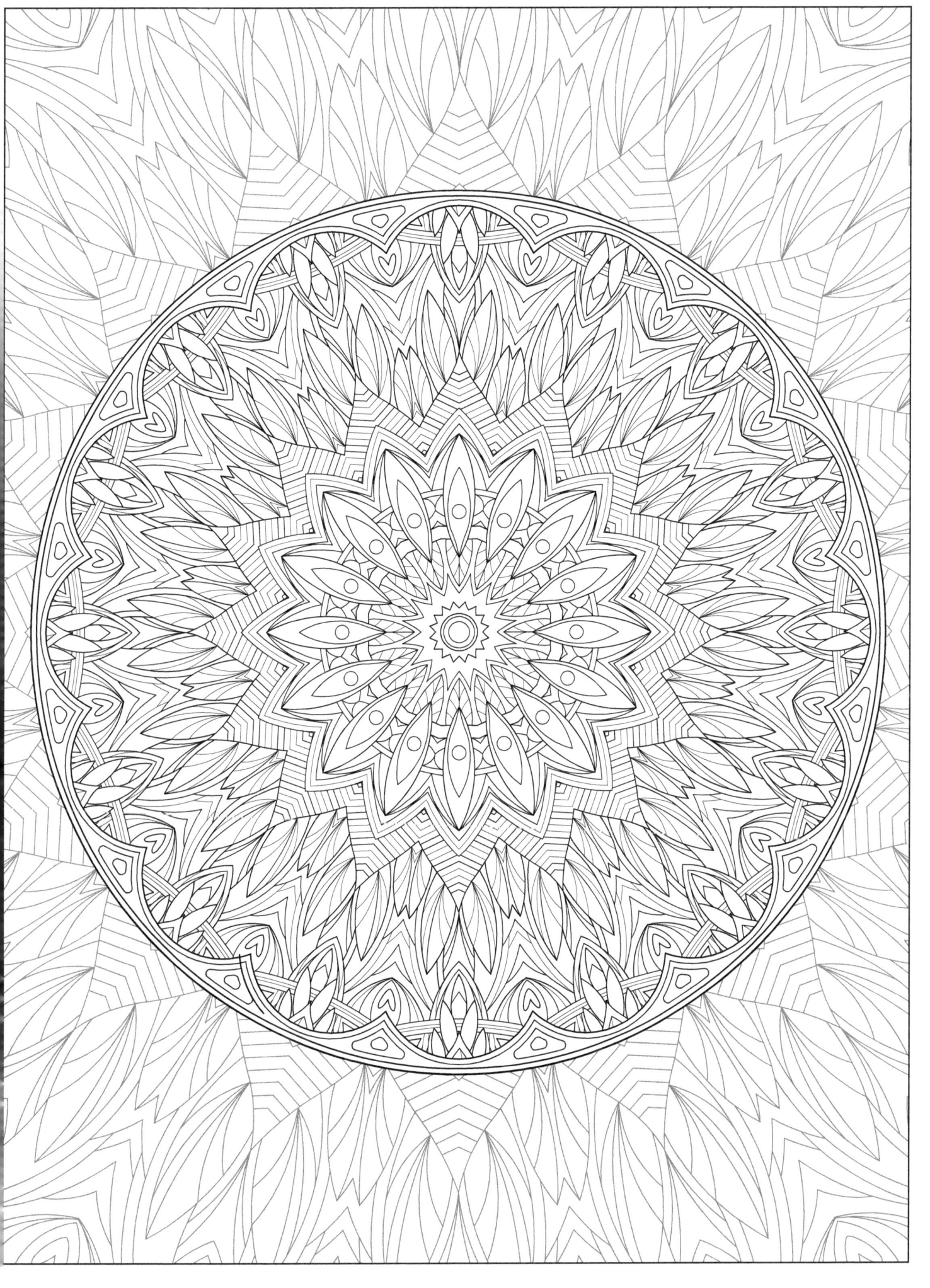

www.ingramcontent.com/pod-product-compliance
Lightning Source LLC
Chambersburg PA
CBHW081826170526
45167CB00007B/2735